# Healthy Eats

**Publisher & Creative Director:** Nick Wells
**Project Editor:** Sarah Goulding
**Designer:** Mike Spender
**With thanks to:** Gina Steer

This is a **FLAME TREE** Book

**FLAME TREE PUBLISHING**
Crabtree Hall, Crabtree Lane
Fulham, London SW6 6TY
United Kingdom
www.flametreepublishing.com

Flame Tree is part of The Foundry Creative Media Company Limited

First published 2005

05 07 09 08 06
1 3 5 7 9 10 8 6 4 2

ISBN 1 84451 334 3

A copy of the CIP data for this book is available from the British Library.

Printed in China

# Healthy Eats

## Quick and Easy Recipes

**FLAME TREE
PUBLISHING**

# Contents

# *Light Bites* **78**

# *Main Meals* **136**

# Vegetarian

# Dinner Parties & Entertaining

## *Puddings & Desserts*

# Store Cupboard Essentials
## Low Fat Ingredients for a Healthy Lifestyle

**Low fat cooking has often been associated with the stigma that reducing fat reduces flavour. This simply is not the case, which is great news for those choosing a lower-fat diet.**

The store cupboard is a good place to start when cooking low fat meals. It is always a good idea, especially when following a low fat diet, to have some well thought out basics in the cupboard – foods that are high on flavour and low in fat.

As store cupboard ingredients keep reasonably well, it really is worth making a trip to a good speciality grocery shop.

If the grocers or local supermarket only carries a limited choice of products, do not despair. The Internet now offers freedom to the food shopaholics amongst us. There are some fantastic food sites, both local and international, where food can be purchased and delivery arranged online.

When thinking about essentials, think of flavour, something that is going to add to a dish without increasing its fat content. It is worth spending a little bit more money on these products to make flavoursome dishes that will help stop the urge to snack on fatty foods.

**COUSCOUS** A precooked wheat semolina. Traditional couscous needs to be steamed and is available from health food stores. This type of couscous contains more nutrients than the instant variety which just needs to be covered with boiling water.

**DRIED FRUIT** The ready-to-eat variety are particularly good as they are plump, juicy and do not need to be soaked. They are fantastic when puréed into a compote, added to water and heated to make a pie filling and when added to stuffing mixtures. They are also good cooked with meats, rice or couscous.

**FLOURS** A useful addition (particularly cornflour) which can be used to thicken sauces. While not strictly a flour, cornmeal is a very versatile low fat ingredient, which can be used when making dumplings and gnocchi.

**NOODLES** Noodles are also very useful and can accompany any Far Eastern dish. They are low fat and also available in the wholewheat variety. Rice noodles are available for those who have gluten-free diets and, like pasta noodles, provide slow-release energy to the body.

**PASTA** Whether fresh or dried, pasta is a versatile ingredient which provides the body with slow-release energy. It comes in many different sizes and shapes; from the tiny tubettini to the larger cannelloni and lasagne sheets.

**BARLEY** A cereal low in gluten, which is chiefly used in soups and stews.

**PULSES** High in nutritional value and a good source of slow-release carbohydrate as well as protein. They come in two forms; either dried (in which case they generally need to be soaked overnight and then cooked before use – it is important to follow the instructions on the back of the packet), or canned. If buying canned pulses, try to buy the variety in water with no added salt or sugar. These simply need to be drained and rinsed before being added to a dish.

Kidney borlotti, cannellini, butter and flageolet beans, split peas and lentils, all make tasty additions to any dish. Baked beans are a favourite with everyone and many shops now stock the organic variety, which have no added salt or sugar but are sweetened with fruit juice instead.

When boiling previously dried pulses, remember that salt should not be added as this will make the skins tough and inedible. Puy lentils are a smaller variety of lentil. They often have mottled skins and are good for cooking in slow dishes as they hold their shape and firm texture particularly well.

**RICE** Basmati and Thai fragrant rice are well suited to Thai and Indian curries as the fine grains absorb the sauce and their delicate creaminess balances the pungency of the spices. Arborio is only one type of risotto rice. Many are available depending on whether the risotto is meant to accompany meat, fish or vegetable dishes. When cooked, rice swells to create a substantial low fat dish. Easy-cook American rice, both plain and wholegrain, is great for casseroles and for stuffing meat, fish and vegetables as it holds its shape and firmness. Pudding rice can be used in a variety of ways to create an irresistible dessert.

**STOCK AND SAUCE BASES** Good quality stock is a must in low fat cooking as it provides a good flavour base for many dishes. Many supermarkets now carry a variety of fresh and organic stocks. There is also a fairly large range of dried stock, perhaps the best being bouillon, a high-quality form of stock (available in powder or liquid form) which can be added to any dish whether it be a sauce, casserole, pie or soup.

A good quality passata sauce or canned plum tomatoes can act as the foundation for any sauce, as can a good quality green or red pesto. Other handy store cupboard additions include tapenade, mustard and anchovies. These ingredients have very distinctive tastes and are particularly flavoursome. Roasted red pepper sauce and sundried tomato purée, which tends to be sweeter and more intensely flavoured than regular tomato purée, are also very useful.

Using herbs when cooking at home should reduce the temptation to buy ready-made sauces. Often these types of sauces contain large amounts of sugar and additives.

Eastern flavours offer a lot of scope where low fat cooking is concerned. Flavourings such as fish sauce, soy sauce, red and green curry paste and Chinese rice wine all offer mouthwatering low fat flavours to any dish.

# Nutrition
## The Role of Essential Nutrients

A healthy and well-balanced diet is the body's primary energy source. In children, it constitutes the building blocks for future health as well as providing lots of energy. In adults, it encourages self-healing and regeneration within the body. A well-balanced diet will provide the body with all the essential nutrients it needs. This can be achieved by eating a variety of foods, demonstrated in the pyramid below:

*Fats*
milk, yogurt
and cheese

*Proteins*
meat, fish, poultry, eggs,
nuts and pulses

*Fruits and
Vegetables*

*Starchy Carbohydrates*
cereals, potatoes, bread, rice and pasta

## Fats

Fats fall into two categories: saturated and unsaturated fats. It is very important that a healthy balance is achieved within the diet. Fats are an essential part of the diet and a source of energy and provide essential fatty acids and fat soluble vitamins. The right balance of fats should boost the body's immunity to infection and keep muscles, nerves and arteries in good condition. Saturated fats are of animal origin and are hard when stored at room temperature. They can be found in dairy produce, meat, eggs, margarines and hard white cooking fat (lard) as well as in manufactured products such as pies, biscuits and cakes. A high intake of saturated fat over many years has been proven to increase heart disease and high blood cholesterol levels and often leads to weight gain. The aim of a healthy diet is to keep the fat content low in the foods that we eat. Lowering the amount of saturated fat that we consume is very important, but this does not mean that it is good to consume lots of other types of fat.

There are two kinds of unsaturated fats: poly-unsaturated fats and monounsaturated fats. Poly-unsaturated fats include the following oils: safflower oil, soybean oil, corn oil and sesame oil. Within the polyunsaturated group are Omega oils. The Omega-3 oils are of significant interest because they have been found to be particularly beneficial to coronary health and can encourage brain growth and development. Omega-3 oils are derived from oily fish such as salmon, mackerel, herring, pilchards and sardines. It is recommended that we should eat these types of fish at least once a week. However, for those who do not eat fish or who are vegetarians, liver oil supplements are available in most supermarkers and health shops. It is suggested that these supplements should be taken on a daily basis. The most popular oils that are high in monounsaturates are olive oil, sunflower oil and peanut oil. The Mediterranean diet which is based on a diet high in mono-unsaturated fats is recommended for heart health. Also, monounsaturated fats are known to help reduce the levels of LDL (the bad) cholestrol.

# Proteins

Composed of amino acids (proteins' building bricks), proteins perform a wide variety of essential functions for the body including supplying energy and building and repairing tissues. Good sources of proteins are eggs, milk, yogurt, cheese, meat, fish, poultry, eggs, nuts and pulses. (See the second level of the pyramid.) Some of these foods, however, contain saturated fats. To strike a nutritional balance eat generous amounts of vegetable protein foods such as soya, beans, lentils, peas and nuts.

# Fruits and Vegetables

Not only are fruits and vegetables the most visually appealing foods, but they are extremely good for us, providing essential vitamins and minerals essential for growth, repair and protection in the human body. Fruits and vegetables are low in calories and

are responsible for regulating the body's metabolic processes and controlling the composition of its fluids and cells.

## Minerals

**CALCIUM** Important for healthy bones and teeth, nerve transmission, muscle contraction, blood clotting and hormone function. Calcium promotes a healthy heart, improves skin, relieves aching muscles and bones, maintains the correct acid-alkaline balance and reduces menstrual cramps. Good sources are dairy products, small bones of small fish, nuts, pulses, fortified white flours, breads and green leafy vegetables.

**CHROMIUM** Part of the glucose tolerance factor, chromium balances blood sugar levels, helps to normalise hunger and reduce cravings, improves lifespan, helps protect DNA and is essential for heart function. Good sources are brewer's yeast, wholemeal bread, rye bread, oysters, potatoes, green peppers, butter and parsnips.

**IODINE** Important for the manufacture of thyroid hormones and for normal development. Good sources of iodine are seafood, seaweed, milk and dairy products.

**IRON** As a component of haemoglobin, iron carries oxygen around the body. It is vital for normal growth and development. Good sources are liver, corned beef, red meat, fortified breakfast cereals, pulses, green leafy vegetables, egg yolk and cocoa and cocoa products.

**MAGNESIUM** Important for efficient functioning of metabolic enzymes and development of the skeleton. Magnesium promotes healthy muscles by helping them to relax and is therefore good for PMS. It is also important for heart muscles and the nervous system. Good sources are nuts, green vegetables, meat, cereals, milk and yogurt.

**PHOSPHORUS** Forms and maintains bones and teeth, builds muscle tissue, helps maintain pH of the body aids metabolism and energy production. Phosphorus is present in almost all foods.

**POTASSIUM** Enables nutrients to move into cells, while waste products move out; promotes healthy nerves and muscles; maintains fluid balance in the body; helps secretion of insulin for blood sugar control to produce constant energy; relaxes muscles; maintains heart functioning and stimulates gut movement to encourage proper elimination. Good sources are fruit, vegetables, milk and bread.

**SELENIUM** Antioxidant properties help to protect against free radicals and carcinogens. Selenium reduces inflammation, stimulates the immune system to fight infections, promotes a healthy heart and helps vitamin E's action. It is also required for the male reproductive system and is needed for metabolism. Good sources are tuna, liver, kidney, meat, eggs, cereals, nuts and dairy products.

**SODIUM** Important in helping to control body fluid and balance, preventing dehydration. Sodium is involved in muscle and nerve function and helps move nutrients into cells. All foods are good sources, however processed, pickled and salted foods are richest in sodium.

**ZINC** Important for metabolism and the healing of wounds. It also aids ability to cope with stress, promotes a healthy

nervous system and brain especially in the growing foetus, aids bones and teeth formation and is essential for constant energy. Good sources are liver, meat, pulses, whole-grain cereals, nuts and oysters.

## Vitamins

**VITAMIN A** Important for cell growth and developmemt and for the formation of visual pigments in the eye. Vitamin A comes in two forms: retinol and beta-carotenes. Retinol is found in liver, meat and meat products and whole milk and its products. Beta-carotene is a powerul antioxidant and is found in red and yellow fruits and vegetables such as carrots, mangoes and apricots.

**VITAMIN B1** Important in releasing energy from carboydrate-containing foods. Good sources are yeast and yeast products, bread, fortified breakfast cereals and potatoes.

**VITAMIN B2** Important for metabolism of proteins, fats and carbohydrates to produce energy. Good sources are meat, yeast extracts, fortified breakfast cereals and milk and its products.

**VITAMIN B3** Required for the metabolism of food into energy production. Good sources are milk and milk products, fortified breakfast cereals, pulses, meat, poultry and eggs.

**VITAMIN B5** Important for the metabolism of food and energy production. All foods are good sources but especially fortified breakfast cereals, whole-grain bread and dairy products.

**VITAMIN B6** Important for metabolism of protein and fat. Vitamin B6 may also be involved with the regulation of sex hormones. Good sources are liver, fish, pork, soya beans and peanuts.

**VITAMIN B12** Important for the production of red blood cells and DNA. It is vital for growth and the nervous system. Good sources are meat, fish, eggs, poultry and milk.

**BIOTIN** Important for metabolism of fatty acids. Good sources of biotin are liver, kidney, eggs and nuts. Micro-organisms also manufacture this vitamin in the gut.

**VITAMIN C** Important for healing wounds and the formation of collagen which keeps skin and bones strong. It is an important antioxidant. Good sources are fruits, soft summer fruits and vegetables.

**VITAMIN D** Important for absorption and handling of calcium to help build bone strength. Good sources are oily fish, eggs, whole milk and milk products, margarine and of course sufficient exposure to sunlight, as vitamin D is made in the skin.

**VITAMIN E** Important as an antioxidant vitamin helping to protect cell membranes from damage. Good sources are vegetable oils, margarines, seeds, nuts and green vegetables.

**FOLIC ACID** Critical during pregnancy for the development of the brain and nerves. It is always essential for brain and nerve function and is needed for utilising protein and red blood cell formation. Good sources are whole-grain cereals, fortified breakfast cereals, green leafy vegetables, oranges and liver.

**VITAMIN K** Important for controlling blood clotting. Good sources are cauliflower, Brussels sprouts, lettuce, cabbage, beans, broccoli, peas, asparagus, potatoes, corn oil, tomatoes and milk.

# Carbohydrates

Carbohydrates are an energy source and come in two forms: starch and sugar. Starch carbohydrates are also known as complex carbohydrates and they include all cereals, potatoes, breads, rice and pasta. (See the fourth level of the pyramid). Eating wholegrain varieties of these foods also provides fibre. Diets high in fibre are believed to be beneficial in helping to prevent bowel cancer and can also keep cholesterol down. High-fibre diets are also good for those concerned about weight gain. Fibre is bulky and fills the stomach, therefore reducing hunger pangs. Sugar carbohydrates, which are also known as fast-release carbohydrates because of the quick fix of energy they give to the body, include sugar and sugar-sweetened products such as jams and syrups. Milk provides lactose which is a milk sugar and fruits provide fructose which is a fruit sugar.

# Soups & Starters

# Mushroom & Sherry Soup

**SERVES 4**

4 slices day old white bread
zest of ½ lemon
1 tbsp lemon juice
salt and freshly ground
   black pepper
125 g/4 oz assorted wild

  mushrooms, lightly rinsed
125 g/4 oz baby button
  mushrooms, wiped
2 tsp olive oil
1 garlic clove, peeled
  and crushed

6 spring onions, trimmed
  and diagonally sliced
600 ml/1 pint chicken stock
4 tbsp dry sherry
1 tbsp freshly snipped
  chives, to garnish

Preheat the oven to 180°C/350°F/Gas Mark 4. Remove the crusts from the bread and cut the bread into small cubes.

In a large bowl toss the cubes of bread with the lemon rind and juice, 2 tablespoons of water and plenty of freshly ground black pepper.

Spread the bread cubes on to a lightly oiled, large baking tray and bake for 20 minutes until golden and crisp.

If the wild mushrooms are small, leave some whole. Otherwise, thinly slice all the mushrooms and reserve.

Heat the oil in a saucepan. Add the garlic and spring onions and cook for 1–2 minutes. Add the mushrooms and cook for 3–4 minutes until they start to soften. Add the chicken stock and stir to mix.

Bring to the boil, then reduce the heat to a gentle simmer. Cover and cook for 10 minutes. Stir in the sherry, and season to taste with a little salt and pepper. Pour into warmed bowls, sprinkle over the chives, and serve immediately with the lemon croûtons.

*Try this:* MAIN MEAL: 152 PUDDING: 360

# Chinese Chicken Soup

**SERVES 4**

225 g/8 oz cooked chicken
1 tsp oil
6 spring onions, trimmed
  and diagonally sliced
1 red chilli, deseeded and
  finely chopped
1 garlic clove, peeled

and crushed
2.5 cm/1 inch piece root
  ginger, peeled and
finely grated
1 litre/1¾ pint chicken stock
150 g/5 oz medium
  egg noodles

1 carrot, peeled and cut
into matchsticks
125 g/4 oz beansprouts
2 tbsp soy sauce
1 tbs p fish sauce
fresh coriander leaves,
  to garnish

Remove any skin from the chicken. Place on a chopping board and use two forks to tear the chicken into fine shreds.

Heat the oil in a large saucepan and fry the spring onions and chilli for 1 minute.

Add the garlic and ginger and cook for another minute.

Stir in the chicken stock and gradually bring the mixture to the boil.

Break up the noodles a little and add to the boiling stock with the carrot. Stir to mix, then reduce the heat to a simmer and cook for 3–4 minutes.

Add the shredded chicken, beansprouts, soy sauce and fish sauce and stir. Cook for a further 2–3 minutes until piping hot. Ladle the soup into bowls and sprinkle with the coriander leaves. Serve immediately.

*Try this:* MAIN MEAL: 138  PUDDING: 378

# Swede, Turnip, Parsnip & Potato Soup

2 large onions, peeled
25 g/1 oz butter
2 medium carrots, peeled and roughly chopped
175 g/6 oz swede, peeled and roughly chopped
125 g/4 oz turnip, peeled and roughly chopped
125 g/4 oz parsnips, peeled and roughly chopped
175 g/6 oz potatoes, peeled
1 litre/1¾ pints vegetable stock
½ tsp freshly grated nutmeg
salt and freshly ground black pepper
4 tbsp vegetable oil, for frying
125 ml/4 fl oz double cream
warm crusty bread, to serve

Finely chop 1 onion. Melt the butter in a large saucepan and add the onion, carrots, swede, turnip, parsnip and potatoes. Cover and cook gently for about 10 minutes, without colouring. Stir occasionally during this time.

Add the stock and season to taste with the nutmeg, salt and pepper. Cover and bring to the boil, then reduce the heat and simmer gently for 15–20 minutes, or until the vegetables are tender. Remove from the heat and leave to cool for 30 minutes.

Heat the oil in a large heavy-based frying pan. Add the onions and cook over a medium heat, for about 2–3 minutes, stirring frequently, until golden brown. Remove the onions with a slotted spoon and drain well on absorbent kitchen paper. As they cool, they will turn crispy. Pour the cooled soup into a food processor or blender and process to form a smooth purée. Return to the cleaned pan, adjust the seasoning, then stir in the cream. Gently reheat and top with the crispy onions. Serve immediately with chunks of bread.

*Try this:* MAIN MEAL: 140  PUDDING: 374

# Carrot & Ginger Soup

**SERVES 4**

4 slices of bread,
crusts removed
1 tsp yeast extract
2 tsp olive oil
1 onion, peeled and chopped
1 garlic clove, peeled
    and crushed
½ tsp ground ginger

450 g/1 lb carrots, peeled
    and chopped
1 litre/1¾ pint
vegetable stock
2.5 cm/1 inch piece of root
    ginger, peeled and
    finely grated
salt and freshly ground

black pepper
1 tbsp lemon juice

To garnish:
chives
lemon zest

Preheat the oven to 180°C/350°F/Gas Mark 4. Roughly chop the bread. Dissolve the yeast extract in 2 tablespoons of warm water and mix with the bread.

Spread the bread cubes over a lightly oiled baking tray and bake for 20 minutes, turning half way through. Remove from the oven and reserve.

Heat the oil in a large saucepan. Gently cook the onion and garlic for 3–4 minutes.

Stir in the ground ginger and cook for 1 minute to release the flavour.

Add the chopped carrots, then stir in the stock and the fresh ginger. Simmer gently for 15 minutes.

Remove from the heat and allow to cool a little. Blend until smooth, then season to taste with salt and pepper. Stir in the lemon juice. Garnish with the chives and lemon zest and serve immediately.

# Potato, Leek & Rosemary Soup

**SERVES 4**

50 g/2 oz butter
450 g/1 lb leeks, trimmed
and finely sliced
700 g/1½ lb potatoes,
peeled and
roughly chopped

900 ml/1½ pints
vegetable stock
4 sprigs of fresh rosemary
450 ml/¾ pint full-
cream milk
2 tbsp freshly

chopped parsley
2 tbsp crème fraîche
salt and freshly ground
black pepper
wholemeal rolls,
to serve

Melt the butter in a large saucepan, add the leeks and cook gently for 5 minutes, stirring frequently. Remove 1 tablespoon of the cooked leeks and reserve for garnishing.

Add the potatoes, vegetable stock, rosemary sprigs and milk. Bring to the boil, then reduce the heat, cover and simmer gently for 20–25 minutes, or until the vegetables are tender.

Cool for 10 minutes. Discard the rosemary, then pour into a food processor or blender and blend well to form a smooth-textured soup.

Return the soup to the cleaned saucepan and stir in the chopped parsley and crème fraîche. Season to taste with salt and pepper. If the soup is too thick, stir in a little more milk or water. Reheat gently without boiling, then ladle into warm soup bowls. Garnish the soup with the reserved leeks and serve immediately with wholemeal rolls.

*Try this:* MAIN MEAL: 154  PUDDING: 352

# Italian Bean Soup

**SERVES 4**

2 tsp olive oil
1 leek, washed and chopped
1 garlic clove, peeled and
  crushed
2 tsp dried oregano
75 g/3 oz green beans,

trimmed and cut into bite-
  size pieces
410 g can cannellini beans,
  drained and rinsed
75 g/3 oz small pasta shapes
1 litre/1¾ pint

vegetable stock
8 cherry tomatoes
salt and freshly ground
  black pepper
3 tbsp freshly
  shredded basil

Heat the oil in a large saucepan. Add the leek, garlic and oregano and cook gently for 5 minutes, stirring occasionally.

Stir in the green beans and the cannellini beans. Sprinkle in the pasta and pour in the stock.

Bring the stock mixture to the boil, then reduce the heat to a simmer.

Cook for 12–15 minutes or until the vegetables are tender and the pasta is cooked to al dente. Stir occasionally.

In a heavy-based frying pan, dry-fry the tomatoes over a high heat until they soften and the skins begin to blacken.

Gently crush the tomatoes in the pan with the back of a spoon and add to the soup.

Season to taste with salt and pepper. Stir in the shredded basil and serve immediately.

*Try this:* MAIN MEAL: 96  PUDDING: 362

# Tomato & Basil Soup

**SERVES 4**

| | | |
|---|---|---|
| 1.1 kg/ 2½ lb ripe tomatoes, cut in half | 1 tbsp dark brown sugar | 2 tbsp freshly chopped basil |
| 2 garlic cloves | 1 tbsp tomato purée | salt and freshly ground black pepper |
| 1 tsp olive oil | 300 ml/½ pint vegetable stock | small basil leaves, to garnish |
| 1 tbsp balsamic vinegar | 6 tbsp low-fat natural yogurt | |

Preheat the oven to 200°C/400°F/Gas Mark 6. Evenly spread the tomatoes and unpeeled garlic in a single layer in a large roasting tin.

Mix the oil and vinegar together. Drizzle over the tomatoes and sprinkle with the dark brown sugar. Roast the tomatoes in the preheated oven for 20 minutes until tender and lightly charred in places.

Remove from the oven and allow to cool slightly. When cool enough to handle, squeeze the softened flesh of the garlic from the papery skin. Place with the charred tomatoes in a nylon sieve over a saucepan. Press the garlic and tomato through the sieve with the back of a wooden spoon.

When all the flesh has been sieved, add the tomato purée and vegetable stock to the pan. Heat gently, stirring occasionally.

In a small bowl beat the yogurt and basil together and season to taste with salt and pepper. Stir the basil yogurt into the soup. Garnish with basil leaves and serve immediately.

*Try this:* MAIN MEAL: 148   PUDDING: 358

# Prawn & Chilli Soup

**SERVES 4**

2 spring onions, trimmed
225 g/8 oz whole raw tiger
   prawns
750 ml/1¼ pint fish stock
finely grated rind and juice

   of 1 lime
1 tbsp fish sauce
1 red chilli, deseeded
   and chopped
1 tbsp soy sauce

1 lemon grass stalk
2 tbsp rice vinegar
4 tbsp freshly
   chopped coriander

To make spring onion curls, finely shred the spring onions lengthways. Place in a bowl of iced cold water and reserve.

Remove the heads and shells from the prawns leaving the tails intact. Split the prawns almost in two to form a butterfly shape and individually remove the black thread that runs down the back of each one.

In a large pan heat the stock with the lime rind and juice, fish sauce, chilli and soy sauce. Bruise the lemon grass by crushing it along its length with a rolling pin, then add to the stock mixture.

When the stock mixture is boiling add the prawns and cook until they are pink. Remove the lemon grass and add the rice vinegar and coriander.

Ladle into bowls and garnish with the spring onion curls. Serve immediately.

*Try this:* MAIN MEAL: 166  PUDDING: 380

# Curried Parsnip Soup

1 tsp cumin seeds
2 tsp coriander seeds
1 tsp oil
1 onion, peeled and chopped
1 garlic clove, peeled
   and crushed
½ tsp turmeric

¼ tsp chilli powder
1 cinnamon stick
450 g/1 lb parsnips, peeled
   and chopped
1 litre/1¾ pint
   vegetable stock
salt and freshly ground

black pepper
2–3 tbsp low-fat natural
   yogurt, to serve
fresh coriander leaves,
   to garnish

In a small frying pan, dry-fry the cumin and coriander seeds over a moderately high heat for 1–2 minutes. Shake the pan during cooking until the seeds are lightly toasted.

Reserve until cooled. Grind the toasted seeds in a pestle and mortar.

Heat the oil in a saucepan. Cook the onion until softened and starting to turn golden. Add the garlic, turmeric, chilli powder and cinnamon stick to the pan. Continue to cook for a further minute.

Add the parsnips and stir well. Pour in the stock and bring to the boil. Cover and simmer for 15 minutes or until the parsnips are cooked.

Allow the soup to cool. Once cooled, remove the cinnamon stick and discard. Blend the soup in a food processor until very smooth.

Transfer to a saucepan and reheat gently. Season to taste with salt and pepper. Garnish with fresh coriander and serve immediately with the yogurt.

*Try this:* MAIN MEAL: 146   PUDDING: 354

# Cream of Spinach Soup

**SERVES 6-8**

1 large onion, peeled
   and chopped
5 large plump garlic cloves,
   peeled and chopped
2 medium potatoes, peeled
   and chopped
750 ml/1¼ pints cold water

1 tsp salt
450 g/1 lb spinach, washed
   and large stems removed
50 g/2 oz butter
3 tbsp flour
750 ml/1¼ pints milk
½ tsp freshly grated nutmeg

freshly ground black pepper
6–8 tbsp crème fraîche or
   soured cream
warm foccacia bread,
   to serve

Place the onion, garlic and potatoes in a large saucepan and cover with the cold water. Add half the salt and bring to the boil. Cover and simmer for 15–20 minutes, or until the potatoes are tender. Remove from the heat and add the spinach. Cover and set aside for 10 minutes.

Slowly melt the butter in another saucepan, add the flour and cook over a low heat for about 2 minutes. Remove the saucepan from the heat and add the milk, a little at a time, stirring continuously. Return to the heat and cook, stirring continuously, for 5–8 minutes, or until the sauce is smooth and slightly thickened. Add the freshly grated nutmeg, or to taste.

Blend the cooled potato and spinach mixture in a food processor or blender to a smooth purée, then return to the saucepan and gradually stir in the white sauce. Season to taste with salt and pepper and gently reheat, taking care not to allow the soup to boil. Ladle into soup bowls and top with spoonfuls of crème fraîche or soured cream. Serve immediately with warm foccacia bread.

*Try this:* MAIN MEAL: 165   PUDDING: 352

# Hot & Sour Mushroom Soup

**SERVES 4**

4 tbsp sunflower oil
3 garlic cloves, peeled and
    finely chopped
3 shallots, peeled and
    finely chopped
2 large red chillies, deseeded
    and finely chopped
1 tbsp soft brown sugar
large pinch of salt

1 litre/1¾ pints
    vegetable stock
250 g/9 oz Thai fragrant rice
5 kaffir lime leaves, torn
2 tbsp soy sauce
grated rind and juice
    of 1 lemon
250 g/9 oz oyster
    mushrooms, wiped and

cut into pieces
2 tbsp freshly
    chopped coriander

To garnish:
2 green chillies, deseeded
    and finely chopped
3 spring onions, trimmed
    and finely chopped

Heat the oil in a frying pan, add the garlic and shallots and cook until golden brown and starting to crisp. Remove from the pan and reserve. Add the chillies to the pan and cook until they start to change colour.

Place the garlic, shallots and chillies in a food processor or blender and blend to a smooth purée with 150 ml/¼ pint water. Pour the purée back into the pan, add the sugar with a large pinch of salt, then cook gently, stirring, until dark in colour. Take care not to burn the mixture.

Pour the stock into a large saucepan, add the garlic purée, rice, lime leaves, soy sauce and the lemon rind and juice. Bring to the boil, then reduce the heat, cover and simmer gently for about 10 minutes.

Add the mushrooms and simmer for a further 10 minutes, or until the mushrooms and rice are tender. Remove the lime leaves, stir in the chopped coriander and ladle into bowls. Place the chopped green chillies and spring onions in small bowls and serve separately to sprinkle on top of the soup.

*Try this:* MAIN MEAL: 204  PUDDING: 362

# Pumpkin & Smoked Haddock Soup

**SERVES 4-6**

2 tbsp olive oil
1 medium onion, peeled
    and chopped
2 garlic cloves, peeled
    and chopped
3 celery stalks, trimmed
    and chopped

700 g/1½ lb pumpkin,
    peeled, deseeded and cut
    into chunks
450 g/1 lb potatoes, peeled
    and cut into chunks
750 ml/1¼ pints chicken
    stock, heated

125 ml/4 fl oz dry sherry
200 g/7 oz smoked
    haddock fillet
150 ml/¼ pint milk
freshly ground black pepper
2 tbsp freshly
    chopped parsley

Heat the oil in a large, heavy-based saucepan and gently cook the onion, garlic, and celery for about 10 minutes. This will release the sweetness but not colour the vegetables. Add the pumpkin and potatoes to the saucepan and stir to coat the vegetables with the oil.

Gradually pour in the stock and bring to the boil. Cover, then reduce the heat and simmer for 25 minutes, stirring occasionally. Stir in the dry sherry, then remove the saucepan from the heat and leave to cool for 5–10 minutes.

Blend the mixture in a food processor or blender to form a chunky purée and return to the cleaned saucepan.

4Meanwhile, place the fish in a shallow frying pan. Pour in the milk with 3 tablespoons of water and bring to almost boiling point. Reduce the heat, cover and simmer for 6 minutes, or until the fish is cooked and flakes easily. Remove from the heat and, using a slotted spoon remove the fish from the liquid, reserving both liquid and fish.

Discard the skin and any bones from the fish and flake into pieces. Stir the fish liquid into the soup, together with the flaked fish. Season with freshly ground black pepper, stir in the parsley and serve immediately.

*Try this:* MAIN MEAL: 190  PUDDING: 366

# Roasted Red Pepper, Tomato & Red Onion Soup

**SERVES 4**

fine spray of oil
2 large red peppers, deseeded and roughly chopped
1 red onion, peeled and roughly chopped
350 g/12 oz tomatoes, halved
1 small crusty French loaf
1 garlic clove, peeled
600 ml/1 pint vegetable stock
salt and freshly ground black pepper
1 tsp Worcestershire sauce
4 tbsp half-fat fromage frais

Preheat the oven to 190°C/375°F/Gas Mark 5. Spray a large roasting tin with the oil and place the peppers and onion in the base. Cook in the oven for 10 minutes. Add the tomatoes and cook for a further 20 minutes or until the peppers are soft.

Cut the bread into 1 cm/½ inch slices. Cut the garlic clove in half and rub the cut edge of the garlic over the bread.

Place all the bread slices on a large baking tray, and bake in the preheated oven for 10 minutes, turning halfway through, until golden and crisp.

Remove the vegetables from the oven and allow to cool slightly, then blend in a food processor until smooth. Strain the vegetable mixture through a large nylon sieve into a saucepan, to remove the seeds and skin. Add the stock, season to taste with salt and pepper and stir to mix. Heat the soup gently until piping hot.

In a small bowl beat together the Worcestershire sauce with the fromage frais.

Pour the soup into warmed bowls and swirl a spoonful of the fromage frais mixture into each bowl. Serve immediately with the garlic toasts.

*Try this:* MAIN MEAL: 230  PUDDING: 358

# Smoked Salmon Sushi

**SERVES 4**

175 g/6 oz sushi rice
2 tbsp rice vinegar
4 tsp caster sugar
½ tsp salt

2 sheets sushi nori
60 g/2½ oz smoked salmon
¼ cucumber, cut into
   fine strips

To serve:
wasabi
soy sauce
pickled ginger

Rinse the rice thoroughly in cold water, until the water runs clear, then place in a pan with 300 ml/½ pint of water. Bring to the boil and cover with a tight-fitting lid. Reduce to a simmer and cook gently for 10 minutes. Turn the heat off, but keep the pan covered, to allow the rice to steam for a further 10 minutes.

In a small saucepan gently heat the rice vinegar, sugar and salt until the sugar has dissolved. When the rice has finished steaming, pour over the vinegar mixture and stir well to mix. Empty the rice out on to a large flat surface – a chopping board or large plate is ideal. Fan the rice to cool and to produce a shinier rice.

Lay one sheet of sushi nori on a sushi mat. If you do not have a sushi mat, improvise with a stiff piece of fabric that is a little larger than the sushi nori. Spread with half the cooled rice – dampen your hands while doing this, as it helps to prevent the rice from sticking to your hands. On the nearest edge place half the salmon and half the cucumber strips.

Roll up the rice and smoked salmon into a tight Swiss roll-like shape. Dampen the blade of a sharp knife and cut the sushi into slices about 2 cm/¾ inch thick. Repeat with the remaining sushi nori, rice, smoked salmon and cucumber. Serve with wasabi, soy sauce and pickled ginger.

*Try this:* MAIN MEAL: 208   PUDDING: 366

# Honey & Ginger Prawns

**SERVES 4**

| | | |
|---|---|---|
| 1 carrot | finely grated | 2 tbsp freshly chopped |
| 50 g/2 oz bamboo shoots | 1 garlic clove, peeled | coriander |
| 4 spring onions | and crushed | salt and freshly ground |
| 1 tbsp clear honey | 1 tbsp lime juice | black pepper |
| 1 tbsp tomato ketchup | 175 g/6 oz peeled prawns, | |
| 1 tsp soy sauce | thawed if frozen | To garnish: |
| 2.5 cm/1 inch piece fresh | 2 heads little gem | fresh coriander sprigs |
| root ginger, peeled and | lettuce leaves | lime slices |

Cut the carrot into matchstick- size pieces, roughly chop the bamboo shoots and finely slice the spring onions.

Combine the bamboo shoots with the carrot matchsticks and spring onions.

In a wok or large frying pan gently heat the honey, tomato ketchup, soy sauce, ginger, garlic and lime juice with 3 tablespoons of water. Bring to the boil.

Add the carrot mixture and stir-fry for 2–3 minutes until the vegetables are hot.

Add the prawns and continue to stir-fry for 2 minutes. Remove the wok or frying pan from the heat and reserve until cooled slightly.

Divide the little gem lettuce into leaves and rinse lightly.

Stir the chopped coriander into the prawn mixture and season to taste with salt and pepper. Spoon into the lettuce leaves and serve immediately garnished with sprigs of fresh coriander and lime slices.

*Try this:* MAIN MEAL: 144  PUDDING: 370

# Rice with Smoked Salmon & Ginger

**SERVES 4**

| | | |
|---|---|---|
| 225 g/8 oz basmati rice | chopped coriander | 1 tsp sesame oil |
| 600 ml/1 pint fish stock | 1 tsp grated fresh | 2 tsp lemon juice |
| 1 bunch spring onions, | root ginger | 4–6 slices pickled ginger |
| trimmed and | 200 g/7 oz sliced smoked | 2 tsp sesame seeds |
| diagonally sliced | salmon | rocket leaves, |
| 3 tbsp freshly | 2 tbsp soy sauce | to serve |

Place the rice in a sieve and rinse under cold water until the water runs clear. Drain, then place in a large saucepan with the stock and bring gently to the boil. Reduce to a simmer and cover with a tight-fitting lid. Cook for 10 minutes, then remove from the heat and leave, covered, for a further 10 minutes.

Stir the spring onions, coriander and fresh ginger into the cooked rice and mix well.

Spoon the rice into four tartlet tins, each measuring 10 cm/4 inches, and press down firmly with the back of a spoon to form cakes. Invert a tin onto an individual serving plate, then tap the base firmly and remove the tin. Repeat with the rest of the filled tins.

Top the rice with the salmon, folding if necessary, so the sides of the rice can still be seen in places. Mix together the soy sauce, sesame oil and lemon juice to make a dressing, then drizzle over the salmon. Top with the pickled ginger and a sprinkling of sesame seeds. Scatter the rocket leaves around the edge of the plates and serve immediately.

*Try this:* MAIN MEAL: 158   PUDDING: 368

# Citrus Monkfish Kebabs

**SERVES 4**

For the marinade:
1 tbsp sunflower oil
finely grated rind and juice
   of 1 lime
1 tbsp lemon juice
1 sprig of freshly
   chopped rosemary

1 tbsp wholegrain mustard
1 garlic clove, peeled
   and crushed
salt and freshly ground
   black pepper

For the kebabs:
450 g/1 lb monkfish tail
8 raw tiger prawns
1 small green courgette,
   trimmed and sliced
4 tbsp of half-fat
   crème fraîche

Preheat the grill and line the grill rack with tinfoil. Mix all the marinade ingredients together in a small bowl and reserve.

Using a sharp knife, cut down both sides of the monkfish tail. Remove the bone and discard. Cut away and discard any skin, then cut the monkfish into bite-sized cubes.

Peel the prawns, leaving the tails intact and remove the thin black vein that runs down the back of each prawn. Place the fish and prawns in a shallow dish.

Pour the marinade over the fish and prawns. Cover lightly and leave to marinate in the refrigerator for 30 minutes. Spoon the marinade over the fish and prawns occasionally during this time. Soak the skewers in cold water for 30 minutes, then drain.

Thread the cubes of fish, prawns and courgettes on to the drained skewers. Arrange on the grill rack then place under the preheated grill and cook for 5–7 minutes, or until cooked thoroughly and the prawns have turned pink. Occasionally brush with the remaining marinade and turn the kebabs during cooking.

Mix 2 tablespoons of the marinade with the crème fraîche and serve as a dip with the kebabs.

*Try this:* MAIN MEAL: 170  PUDDING: 366

# Hot Tiger Prawns with Parma Ham

**SERVES 4**

½ cucumber, peeled if preferred
4 ripe tomatoes
12 raw tiger prawns
6 tbsp olive oil

4 garlic cloves, peeled and crushed
4 tbsp freshly chopped parsley
salt and freshly ground

black pepper
6 slices of Parma ham, cut in half
4 slices flat Italian bread
4 tbsp dry white wine

Preheat the oven to 180˚C/350˚F/Gas Mark 4. Slice the cucumber and tomatoes thinly, then arrange on four large plates and reserve. Peel the prawns, leaving the tail shell intact and remove the thin black vein running down the back.

Whisk together 4 tablespoons of the olive oil, garlic and chopped parsley in a small bowl and season to taste with plenty of salt and pepper. Add the prawns to the mixture and stir until they are well coated. Remove the prawns, then wrap each one in a piece of Parma ham and secure with a cocktail stick.

Place the prepared prawns on a lightly oiled baking sheet or dish with the slices of bread and cook in the preheated oven for 5 minutes.

Remove the prawns from the oven and spoon the wine over the prawns and bread. Return to the oven and cook for a further 10 minutes until piping hot.

Carefully remove the cocktail sticks and arrange three prawn rolls on each slice of bread. Place on top of the sliced cucumber and tomatoes and serve immediately.

*Try this:* MAIN MEAL: 146 PUDDING: 354

# Potato Pancakes with Smoked Salmon

**SERVES 4**

450 g/1 lb floury potatoes,
   peeled and quartered
salt and freshly ground
   black pepper
1 large egg
1 large egg yolk
25 g/1 oz butter

25 g/1 oz plain flour
150 ml/¼ pint double cream
2 tbsp freshly
   chopped parsley
5 tbsp crème fraîche
1 tbsp horseradish sauce
225 g/8 oz smoked

   salmon, sliced
salad leaves,
   to serve

To garnish:
lemon slices
snipped chives

Cook the potatoes in a sauce-pan of lightly salted boiling water for 15–20 minutes, or until tender. Drain thoroughly, then mash until free of lumps. Beat in the whole egg and egg yolk, together with the butter. Beat until smooth and creamy. Slowly beat in the flour and cream, then season to taste with salt and pepper. Stir in the chopped parsley.

Beat the crème fraîche and horseradish sauce together in a small bowl, cover with cling-film and reserve.

Heat a lightly oiled, heavy-based frying pan over a medium-high heat. Place a few spoonfuls of the potato mixture in the hot pan and cook for 4–5 minutes, or until cooked and golden, turning halfway through cooking time. Remove from the pan, drain on absorbent kitchen paper and keep warm. Repeat with the remaining mixture.

Arrange the pancakes on individual serving plates. Place the smoked salmon on the pancakes and spoon over a little of the horseradish sauce. Serve with salad and the remaining horseradish sauce and garnish with lemon slices and chives.

*Try this:* MAIN MEAL: 148  PUDDING: 378

# Seared Scallop Salad

**SERVES 4**

12 king (large) scallops
1 tbsp low-fat spread
   or butter
2 tbsp orange juice

2 tbsp balsamic vinegar
1 tbsp clear honey
2 ripe pears, washed
125 g/4 oz rocket

125 g/4 oz watercress
50 g/2 oz walnuts
freshly ground
   black pepper

Clean the scallops removing the thin black vein from around the white meat and coral. Rinse thoroughly and dry on absorbent kitchen paper. Cut into 2–3 thick slices, depending on the scallop size.

Heat a griddle pan or heavy-based frying pan, then when hot, add the low-fat spread or butter and allow to melt.

Once melted, sear the scallops for 1 minute on each side or until golden. Remove from the pan and reserve.

Briskly whisk together the orange juice, balsamic vinegar and honey to make the dressing and reserve.

With a small, sharp knife carefully cut the pears into quarters, core then cut into chunks.

Mix the rocket leaves, watercress, pear chunks and walnuts. Pile on to serving plates and top with the scallops.

Drizzle over the dressing and grind over plenty of black pepper. Serve immediately.

*Try this:* MAIN MEAL: 170  PUDDING: 364

# Salmon Fish Cakes

**SERVES 4**

225 g/8 oz potatoes, peeled
450 g/1 lb salmon
    fillet, skinned
125 g/4 oz carrot, trimmed
    and peeled
2 tbsp grated lemon rind

2–3 tbsp freshly
    chopped coriander
1 medium egg yolk
salt and freshly ground
    black pepper
2 tbsp plain white flour

few fine sprays of oil

To serve:
prepared tomato sauce
tossed green salad
crusty bread

Cube the potatoes and cook in lightly salted boiling water for 15 minutes. Drain and mash the potatoes. Place in a mixing bowl and reserve.

Place the salmon in a food processor and blend to form a chunky purée. Add the purée to the potatoes and mix together.

Coarsely grate the carrot and add to the fish with the lemon rind and the coriander.

Add the egg yolk, season to taste with salt and pepper, then gently mix the ingredients together. With damp hands form the mixture into four large fish cakes.

Coat in the flour and place on a plate. Cover loosely and chill for at least 30 minutes.

When ready to cook, spray a griddle pan with a few fine sprays of oil and heat the pan. When hot add the fish cakes and cook on both sides for 3–4 minutes or until the fish is cooked. Add an extra spray of oil if needed during the cooking.

When the fish cakes are cooked, serve immediately with the tomato sauce, green salad and crusty bread.

*Try this:* MAIN MEAL: 174  PUDDING: 376

# Wild Rice & Bacon Salad with Smoked Chicken

**SERVES 4**

150 g/5 oz wild rice
50 g/2 oz pecan or
   walnut halves
1 tbsp vegetable oil
4 slices smoked bacon, diced
3–4 shallots, peeled and
finely chopped
75 ml/3 fl oz walnut oil
2–3 tbsp sherry or
   cider vinegar
2 tbsp freshly chopped dill
salt and freshly ground
black pepper
275 g/10 oz smoked
   chicken or duck
   breast, thinly sliced
dill sprigs, to garnish

Put the wild rice in a medium saucepan with 600 ml/1 pint water and bring to the boil, stirring once or twice. Reduce the heat, cover and simmer gently for 30–50 minutes, depending on the texture you prefer, chewy or tender. Using a fork, gently fluff into a large bowl and leave to cool slightly.

Meanwhile, toast the nuts in a frying pan over a medium heat for 2 minutes, or until they are fragrant and lightly coloured,  stirring and tossing frequently. Cool, then chop coarsely and add to the rice.

Heat the oil in the frying pan over a medium heat. Add the bacon and cook, stirring from time to time, for 3–4 minutes, or until crisp and brown. Remove from the pan and drain on absorbent kitchen paper. Add the shallots to the pan and cook for 4 minutes, or until just softened, stirring from time to time. Stir into the rice and nuts, with the drained bacon pieces.

Whisk the walnut oil, vinegar, half the dill and salt and pepper in a small bowl until combined. Pour the dressing over the rice mixture and toss well to combine. Mix the chicken and the remaining chopped dill into the rice, then spoon into bowls and garnish each serving with a dill sprig. Serve slightly warm, or at room temperature.

*Try this:* MAIN MEAL: 140  PUDDING: 372

# Oriental Minced Chicken on Rocket & Tomato

**SERVES 4**

2 shallots, peeled
1 garlic clove, peeled
1 carrot, peeled
50 g/2 oz water chestnuts
1 tsp oil

350 g/12 oz fresh
   chicken mince
1 tsp Chinese
   five-spice powder
pinch chilli powder

1 tsp soy sauce
1 tbsp fish sauce
8 cherry tomatoes
50 g/2 oz rocket

Finely chop the shallots and garlic. Cut the carrot into matchsticks, thinly slice the water chestnuts and reserve. Heat the oil in a wok or heavy-based large frying pan and add the chicken. Stir-fry for 3–4 minutes over a moderately high heat, breaking up any large pieces of chicken.

Add the garlic and shallots and cook for 2–3 minutes until softened. Sprinkle over the Chinese five-spice powder and the chilli powder and continue to cook for about 1 minute.

Add the carrot, water chestnuts, soy and fish sauce and 2 tablespoons of water. Stir-fry for a further 2 minutes. Remove from the heat and reserve to cool slightly.

Deseed the tomatoes and cut into thin wedges. Toss with the rocket and divide between four serving plates. Spoon the warm chicken mixture over the rocket and tomato wedges and serve immediately to prevent the rocket from wilting.

*Try this:* MAIN MEAL: 150  PUDDING: 354

# Mushroom & Red Wine Pâté

**SERVES 4**

3 large slices of white bread, crusts removed
2 tsp oil
1 small onion, peeled and finely chopped
1 garlic clove, peeled and crushed

350 g/12 oz button mushrooms, wiped and finely chopped
150 ml/¼ pint red wine
½ tsp dried mixed herbs
1 tbsp freshly chopped parsley

salt and freshly ground black pepper
2 tbsp low-fat cream cheese

To serve:
finely chopped cucumber
finely chopped tomato

Preheat the oven to 180°C/350°F/Gas Mark 4. Cut the bread in half diagonally. Place the bread triangles on a baking tray and cook for 10 minutes.

Remove from the oven and split each bread triangle in half to make 12 triangles and return to the oven until golden and crisp. Leave to cool on a wire rack.

Heat the oil in a saucepan and gently cook the onion and garlic until transparent.

Add the mushrooms and cook, stirring for 3–4 minutes or until the mushroom juices start to run.

Stir the wine and herbs into the mushroom mixture and bring to the boil. Reduce the heat and simmer uncovered until all the liquid is absorbed.

Remove from the heat and season to taste with salt and pepper. Leave to cool.

When cold, beat in the soft cream cheese and adjust the seasoning. Place in a small clean bowl and chill until required. Serve the toast triangles with the cucumber and tomato.

*Try this:* MAIN MEAL: 240  PUDDING: 374

# Hot Herby Mushrooms

**SERVES 4**

4 thin slices of white bread,
  crusts removed
125 g/4 oz chestnut
  mushrooms, wiped
  and sliced
125 g/4 oz oyster
  mushrooms, wiped

1 garlic clove, peeled
  and crushed
1 tsp Dijon mustard
300 ml/½ pint chicken stock
salt and freshly ground
  black pepper
1 tbsp freshly chopped

parsley
1 tbsp freshly snipped
  chives, plus extra
  to garnish
mixed salad leaves,
  to serve

Preheat the oven to 180°C/350°F/Gas Mark 4. With a rolling pin, roll each piece of bread out as thinly as possible.

Press each piece of bread into a 10 cm/4 inch tartlet tin. Push each piece firmly down, then bake in the preheated oven for 20 minutes.

Place the mushrooms in a frying pan with the garlic, mustard and chicken stock and stir-fry over a moderate heat until the mushrooms are tender and the liquid is reduced by half.

Carefully remove the mushrooms from the frying pan with a slotted spoon and transfer to a heat-resistant dish. Cover with tinfoil and place in the bottom of the oven to keep the mushrooms warm.

Boil the remaining pan juices until reduced to a thick sauce. Season with salt and pepper.

Stir the parsley and the chives into the mushroom mixture.

Place one bread tartlet case on each plate and divide the mushroom mixture between them. Spoon over the pan juices, garnish with the chives and serve immediately with mixed salad leaves.

*Try this:* MAIN MEAL: 138  PUDDING: 358

# Roasted Aubergine Dip with Pitta Strips

**SERVES 4**

4 pitta breads
2 large aubergines
1 garlic clove, peeled
¼ tsp sesame oil

1 tbsp lemon juice
½ tsp ground cumin
salt and freshly ground
   black pepper

2 tbsp freshly
   chopped parsley
fresh salad leaves,
   to serve

Preheat the oven to 180°C/350°F/Gas Mark 4. On a chopping board cut the pitta breads into strips. Spread the bread in a single layer on to a large baking tray.

Cook in the preheated oven for 15 minutes until golden and crisp. Leave to cool on a wire cooling rack.

Trim the aubergines, rinse lightly and reserve. Heat a griddle pan until almost smoking. Cook the aubergines and garlic for about 15 minutes.

Turn the aubergines frequently, until very tender with wrinkled and charred skins. Remove from heat. Leave to cool.

When the aubergines are cool enough to handle, cut in half and scoop out the cooked flesh and place in a food processor.

Squeeze the softened garlic flesh from the papery skin and add to the aubergine.

Blend the aubergine and garlic until smooth, then add the sesame oil, lemon juice and cumin and blend again to mix.

Season to taste with salt and pepper, stir in the parsley and serve with the pitta strips and mixed salad leaves.

*Try this:* MAIN MEAL: 160  PUDDING: 368

# Wild Rice Dolmades

**SERVES 4-6**

6 tbsp olive oil
25 g/1 oz pine nuts
175 g/6 oz mushrooms,
   wiped and finely chopped
4 spring onions, trimmed
   and finely chopped
1 garlic clove, peeled

and crushed
50 g/2 oz cooked wild rice
2 tsp freshly chopped dill
2 tsp freshly chopped mint
salt and freshly ground
   black pepper
16–24 prepared medium

vine leaves
about 300 ml/½ pint
   vegetable stock

To garnish:
lemon wedges
sprigs of fresh dill

Heat 1 tbsp of the oil in a frying pan and gently cook the pine nuts for 2–3 minutes, stirring frequently, until golden. Remove from the pan and reserve.

Add 1½ tablespoons of oil to the pan and gently cook the mushrooms, spring onions and garlic for 7–8 minutes until very soft. Stir in the rice, herbs, salt and pepper.

Put a heaped teaspoon of stuffing in the centre of each leaf (if the leaves are small, put 2 together, overlapping slightly). Fold over the stalk end, then the sides and roll up to make a neat parcel. Continue until all the stuffing is used.

Arrange the stuffed vine leaves close together seam-side down in a large saucepan, drizzling each with a little of the remaining oil – there will be several layers. Pour over just enough stock to cover.

Put an inverted plate over the dolmades to stop them unrolling during cooking. Bring to the boil, then simmer very gently for 3 minutes. Cool in the saucepan.

Transfer the dolmades to a serving dish. Cover and chill in the refrigerator before serving. Sprinkle with the pine nuts and garnish with lemon and dill. Serve.

*Try this:* MAIN MEAL: 192 PUDDING: 380

# Roasted Mixed Vegetables with Garlic & Herb Sauce

**SERVES 4**

1 large garlic bulb
1 large onion, peeled
   and cut into wedges
4 small carrots, peeled
   and quartered
4 small parsnips, peeled
6 small potatoes, scrubbed
   and halved
1 fennel bulb, sliced thickly
4 sprigs of fresh rosemary
4 sprigs of fresh thyme
2 tbsp olive oil
salt and freshly ground
   black pepper
200 g/7 oz low-fat soft
   cheese with herbs
   and garlic
4 tbsp milk
zest of ½ lemon
sprigs of thyme,
   to garnish

Preheat the oven to 220°C/425°F/Gas Mark 7. Cut the garlic in half horizontally. Put into a large roasting tin with all the vegetables and herbs.

Add the oil, season well with salt and pepper and toss together to coat lightly in the oil.

Cover with tinfoil and roast in the preheated oven for 50 minutes. Remove the tinfoil and cook for a further 30 minutes until all the vegetables are tender and slightly charred.

Remove the tin from the oven and allow to cool.

In a small saucepan, melt the low-fat soft cheese together with the milk and lemon zest.

Remove the garlic from the roasting tin and squeeze the flesh into a bowl. Mash thoroughly then add to the sauce. Heat through gently. Season the vegetables to taste. Pour some sauce into small ramekins and garnish with 4 sprigs of thyme. Serve immediately with the roasted vegetables and the sauce to dip.

*Try this:* MAIN MEAL: 142   PUDDING: 352

# Crostini with Chicken Livers

**SERVES 4**

2 tbsp olive oil
2 tbsp butter
1 shallot, peeled and
 finely chopped
1 garlic clove, peeled
 and crushed
150 g/5 oz chicken livers
1 tbsp plain flour

2 tbsp dry white wine
1 tbsp brandy
50 g/2 oz mushrooms, sliced
salt and freshly ground
 black pepper
4 slices of ciabatta or
 similar bread

To garnish:
fresh sage leaves
lemon wedges

Heat 1 tablespoon of the olive oil and 1 tablespoon of the butter in a frying pan, add the shallot and garlic and cook gently for 2–3 minutes.

Trim and wash the chicken livers thoroughly and pat dry on absorbent kitchen paper as much as possible. Cut into slices, then toss in the flour. Add the livers to the frying pan with the shallot and garlic and continue to fry for a further 2 minutes, stirring continuously.

Pour in the white wine and brandy and bring to the boil. Boil rapidly for 1–2 minutes to allow the alcohol to evaporate, then stir in the sliced mushrooms and cook gently for about 5 minutes, or until the chicken livers are cooked, but just a little pink inside. Season to taste with salt and pepper.

Fry the slices of ciabatta or similar-style bread in the remaining oil and butter, then place on individual serving dishes. Spoon over the liver mixture and garnish with a few sage leaves and lemon wedges. Serve immediately.

*Try this:* MAIN MEAL: 172  PUDDING: 362

# Aubergine & Yogurt Dip

**MAKES 600 ml/1 pint**

2 x 225 g/8 oz aubergines
1 tbsp light olive oil
1 tbsp lemon juice
2 garlic cloves, peeled
    and crushed
190 g jar pimentos, drained

150 ml/¼ pint low-fat
    natural yogurt
salt and freshly ground
    black pepper
25 g/1 oz black olives, pitted
    and chopped

225 g/8 oz cauliflower florets
225 g/8 oz broccoli florets
125 g/4 oz carrots, peeled
    and cut into 5 cm/
    2 inch strips

Preheat the oven to 200°C/400°F/Gas Mark 6. Pierce the skin of the aubergines with a fork and place on a baking tray. Cook for 40 minutes or until very soft.

Cool the aubergines, then cut in half, and scoop out the flesh and tip into a bowl.

Mash the aubergine with the olive oil, lemon juice and garlic until smooth or blend for a few seconds in a food processor.

Chop the pimentos into small dice and add to the aubergine mixture. When blended, add the yogurt. Stir well and season to taste with salt and pepper. Add the chopped olives and leave in the refrigerator to chill for at least 30 minutes.

Place the cauliflower and broccoli florets and carrot strips into a pan and cover with boiling water. Simmer for 2 minutes, then rinse in cold water. Drain and serve as crudités to accompany the dip.

*Try this:* MAIN MEAL: 154  PUDDING: 366

# Light Bites

# Thai Crab Cakes

**SERVES 4**

200 g/7 oz easy-cook
  basmati rice
450 ml/¾ pint chicken
  stock, heated
200 g/7 oz cooked crab meat
125 g/4 oz cod fillet, skinned
  and minced
5 spring onions, trimmed
  and finely chopped
1 lemon grass stalk, outer

leaves discarded and
  finely chopped
1 green chilli, deseeded and
  finely chopped
1 tbsp freshly grated
  root ginger
1 tbsp freshly chopped
  coriander
1 tbsp plain flour
1 medium egg

salt and freshly ground
  black pepper
2 tbsp vegetable oil,
  for frying

To serve:
sweet chilli dipping sauce
fresh salad leaves

Put the rice in a large saucepan and add the hot stock. Bring to the boil, cover and simmer over a low heat, without stirring, for 18 minutes, or until the grains are tender and all the liquid is absorbed.

To make the cakes, place the crab meat, fish, spring onions, lemon grass, chilli, ginger, coriander, flour and egg in a food processor. Blend until all the ingredients are mixed thoroughly, then season to taste with salt and pepper. Add the rice to the processor and blend once more, but do not over mix.

Remove the mixture from the processor and place on a clean work surface. With damp hands, divide into 12 even-sized patties. Transfer to a plate, cover and chill in the refrigerator for about 30 minutes.

Heat the oil in a heavy-based frying pan and cook the crab cakes, four at a time, for 3–5 minutes on each side until crisp and golden. Drain on absorbent kitchen paper and serve immediately with a chilli dipping sauce.

*Try this:* MAIN MEAL: 138  PUDDING: 364

# Tuna Chowder

**SERVES 4**

2 tsp oil
1 onion, peeled and
   finely chopped
2 sticks of celery, trimmed
   and finely sliced
1 tbsp plain flour

600 ml/1 pint skimmed milk
200 g can tuna in water
320 g can sweetcorn in
   water, drained
2 tsp freshly chopped thyme
salt and freshly ground

black pepper
pinch cayenne pepper
2 tbsp freshly
   chopped parsley

Heat the oil in a large heavy-based saucepan. Add the onion and celery and gently cook for about 5 minutes, stirring from time to time until the onion is softened.

Stir in the flour and cook for about 1 minute to thicken.

Draw the pan off the heat and gradually pour in the milk, stirring throughout.

Add the tuna and its liquid, the drained sweetcorn and the thyme.

Mix gently, then bring to the boil. Cover and simmer for 5 minutes.

Remove the pan from the heat and season to taste with salt and pepper.

Sprinkle the chowder with the cayenne pepper and chopped parsley. Divide into soup bowls and serve immediately.

*Try this:* MAIN MEAL: 186  PUDDING: 352

# Barbecued Fish Kebabs

**SERVES 4**

450 g/1 lb herring
   or mackerel fillets, cut
   into chunks
2 small red onions, peeled
   and quartered
16 cherry tomatoes

salt and freshly ground
   black pepper

For the sauce:
150 ml /¼ pint fish stock
5 tbsp tomato ketchup

2 tbsp Worcestershire sauce
2 tbsp wine vinegar
2 tbsp brown sugar
2 drops tabasco
2 tbsp tomato purée

Line a grill rack with a single layer of tinfoil and preheat the grill at a high temperature, 2 minutes before use.

If using wooden skewers, soak in cold water for 30 minutes to prevent them from catching alight during cooking.

Meanwhile, prepare the sauce. Add the fish stock, tomato ketchup, Worcestershire sauce, vinegar, sugar, tabasco and tomato purée to a small saucepan. Stir well and leave to simmer for 5 minutes.

When ready to cook, drain the skewers, if necessary, then thread the fish chunks, the quartered red onions and the cherry tomatoes alternately on to the skewers.

Season the kebabs to taste with salt and pepper and brush with the sauce. Grill under the preheated grill for 8–10 minutes, basting with the sauce occasionally during cooking. Turn the kebabs often to ensure that they are cooked thoroughly and evenly on all sides. Serve immediately with couscous.

*Try this:* MAIN MEAL: 200  PUDDING: 370

# Sardines with Redcurrants

**SERVES 4**

2 tbsp redcurrant jelly
finely grated rind of 1 lime
2 tbsp medium dry sherry
450 g /1 lb fresh sardines,
   cleaned and heads

removed
sea salt and freshly
   ground black pepper
lime wedges,
   to garnish

To serve:
fresh redcurrants
fresh green salad

Preheat the grill and line the grill rack with tinfoil 2–3 minutes before cooking.

Warm the redcurrant jelly in a bowl standing over a pan of gently simmering water and stir until smooth. Add the lime rind and sherry to the bowl and stir well until blended.

Lightly rinse the sardines and pat dry with absorbent kitchen paper.

Place on a chopping board and with a sharp knife make several diagonal cuts across the flesh of each fish. Season the sardines inside the cavities with salt and pepper.

Gently brush the warm marinade over the skin and inside the cavities of the sardines.

Place on the grill rack and cook under the preheated grill for 8–10 minutes, or until the fish are cooked.

Carefully turn the sardines over at least once during grilling. Baste occasionally with the remaining redcurrant and lime marinade. Garnish with the redcurrants. Serve immediately with the salad and lime wedges.

*Try this:* MAIN MEAL: 152  PUDDING: 378

# Smoked Haddock Rosti

**SERVES 4**

| | | |
|---|---|---|
| 450 g/1 lb potatoes, peeled and coarsely grated | 450 g/1 lb smoked haddock | chopped parsley |
| 1 large onion, peeled and coarsely grated | 1 tbsp olive oil | 2 tbsp half-fat crème fraîche |
| 2–3 garlic cloves, peeled and crushed | salt and freshly ground black pepper | mixed salad leaves, to garnish |
| | finely grated rind of ½ lemon | lemon wedges, to serve |
| | 1 tbsp freshly | |

Dry the grated potatoes in a clean tea towel. Rinse the grated onion thoroughly in cold water, dry in a clean tea towel and add to the potatoes.

Stir the garlic into the potato mixture. Skin the smoked haddock and remove as many of the tiny pin bones as possible. Cut into thin slices and reserve.

Heat the oil in a non-stick frying pan. Add half the potatoes and press well down in the frying pan. Season to taste with salt and pepper.

Add a layer of fish and a sprinkling of lemon rind, parsley and a little black pepper.

Top with the remaining potatoes and press down firmly. Cover with a sheet of tinfoil and cook on the lowest heat for 25–30 minutes.

Preheat the grill 2–3 minutes before the end of cooking time. Remove the tinfoil and place the rosti under the grill to brown. Turn out on to a warmed serving dish, and serve immediately with spoonfuls of crème fraîche, lemon wedges and mixed salad leaves.

*Try this:* MAIN MEAL: 170  PUDDING: 376

# Sweet & Sour Prawns with Noodles

**SERVES 4**

425 g can pineapple pieces
in natural juice
1 green pepper, deseeded
and cut into quarters
1 tbsp groundnut oil
1 onion, cut into thin wedges
3 tbsp soft brown sugar

150 ml/¼ pint chicken stock
4 tbsp wine vinegar
1 tbsp tomato purée
1 tbsp light soy sauce
1 tbsp cornflour
350 g/12 oz raw tiger
prawns, peeled

225 g/8 oz pak choi,
shredded
350 g/12 oz medium
egg noodles
coriander leaves,
to garnish

Make the sauce by draining the pineapple and reserving 2 tablespoons of the juice.

Remove the membrane from the quartered peppers and cut into thin strips.

Heat the oil in a saucepan. Add the onion and pepper and cook for about 4 minutes or until the onion has softened.

Add the pineapple, the sugar, stock, vinegar, tomato purée and the soy sauce.

Bring the sauce to the boil and simmer for about 4 minutes. Blend the cornflour with the reserved pineapple juice and stir into the pan, stirring until thickened.

Clean the prawns if needed. Wash the pak choi thoroughly, then shred. Add the prawns and pak choi to the sauce. Simmer gently for 3 minutes or until the prawns are cooked and have turned pink.

Cook the noodles in boiling water for 4–5 minutes until just tender.

Drain and arrange the noodles on a warmed plate and pour over the sweet-and-sour prawns. Garnish with coriander leaves and serve immediately.

*Try this:* MAIN MEAL: 146  PUDDING: 370

# Spanish Omelette with Smoked Cod

**SERVES 3-4**

3 tbsp sunflower oil
350 g/12 oz potatoes, peeled
  and cut into 1 cm/½
  inch cubes
2 medium onions, peeled
  and cut into wedges
2–4 large garlic cloves,
  peeled and thinly sliced
1 large red pepper,

deseeded, quartered and
  thinly sliced
125 g/4 oz smoked cod
salt and freshly ground
  black pepper

25 g/1 oz butter, melted
1 tbsp double cream
6 medium eggs, beaten

2 tbsp freshly chopped flat-
  leaf parsley
50 g/2 oz mature Cheddar
  cheese, grated

To serve:
crusty bread
tossed green salad,
  to serve

Heat the oil in a large, non-stick, heavy-based frying pan, add the potatoes, onions and garlic and cook gently for 10–15 minutes until golden brown, then add the red pepper and cook for 3 minutes.

Meanwhile, place the fish in a shallow frying pan and cover with water. Season to taste with salt and pepper and poach gently for 10 minutes. Drain and flake the fish into a bowl, toss in the melted butter and cream, adjust the seasoning and reserve.

When the vegetables are cooked, drain off any excess oil and stir in the beaten egg with the chopped parsley. Pour the fish mixture over the top and cook gently for 5 minutes, or until the eggs become firm.

Sprinkle the grated cheese over the top and place the pan under a preheated hot grill. Cook for 2–3 minutes until the cheese is golden and bubbling. Carefully slide the omelette onto a large plate and serve immediately with plenty of bread and salad.

*Try this:* MAIN MEAL: 186  PUDDING: 352

# Mediterranean Feast

**SERVES 4**

1 small iceberg lettuce
225 g/8 oz French beans
225 g/8 oz baby new
    potatoes, scrubbed
4 medium eggs
1 green pepper
1 medium onion, peeled
200 g can tuna in brine,
    drained and flaked
    into small pieces

50 g/2 oz low-fat hard
    cheese, such as Edam, cut
    into small cubes
8 ripe but firm cherry
    tomatoes, quartered
50 g/2 oz black pitted
    olives, halved
freshly chopped basil,
    to garnish

For the lime vinaigrette:
3 tbsp light olive oil
2 tbsp white wine vinegar
4 tbsp lime juice
grated rind of 1 lime
1 tsp Dijon mustard
1-2 tsp caster sugar
salt and freshly ground
    black pepper

Cut the lettuce into four and remove the hard core. Tear into bite-sized pieces and arrange on a large serving platter or four individual plates.

Cook the French beans in boiling salted water for 8 minutes and the potatoes for 10 minutes or until tender. Drain and rinse in cold water until cool, then cut both the beans and potatoes in half with a sharp knife.

Boil the eggs for 10 minutes, then rinse thoroughly under a cold running tap until cool. Remove the shells under water and cut each egg into four.

Remove the seeds from the pepper and cut into thin strips and finely chop the onion.

Arrange the beans, potatoes, eggs, peppers and onion on top of the lettuce. Add the tuna, cheese and tomatoes. Sprinkle over the olives and garnish with the basil.

To make the vinaigrette, place all the ingredients in a screw-topped jar and shake vigorously until everything is mixed thoroughly. Spoon 4 tablespoons over the top of the prepared salad and serve the remainder separately.

*Try this:* MAIN MEAL: 144 PUDDING: 358

# Smoked Salmon Quiche

**SERVES 6**

225 g/8 oz plain flour
50 g/2 oz butter
50 g/2 oz white vegetable fat
  or lard
2 tsp sunflower oil
225 g/8 oz potato, peeled
  and diced

125 g/4 oz Gruyère
  cheese, grated
75 g/3 oz smoked
  salmon trimmings
5 medium eggs, beaten
300 ml/½ pint single cream
salt and freshly ground

black pepper
1 tbsp freshly chopped
  flat-leaf parsley

To serve:
mixed salad
baby new potatoes

Preheat the oven to 200°C/400°F/Gas Mark 6. Blend the flour, butter and white vegetable fat or lard together until it resembles fine breadcrumbs. Blend again, adding sufficient water to make a firm but pliable dough. Use the dough to line a 23 cm/9 inch flan dish or tin, then chill the pastry case in the refrigerator for 30 minutes. Bake blind with baking beans for 10 minutes.

Heat the oil in a small frying pan, add the diced potato and cook for 3–4 minutes until lightly browned. Reduce the heat and cook for 2–3 minutes, or until tender. Leave to cool.

Scatter the grated cheese evenly over the base of the pastry case, then arrange the cooled potato on top. Add the smoked salmon in an even layer.

Beat the eggs with the cream and season to taste with salt and pepper. Whisk in the parsley and pour the mixture carefully into the dish.

Reduce the oven to 180°C/350°F/Gas Mark 4 and bake for about 30–40 minutes, or until the filling is set and golden. Serve hot or cold with a mixed salad and baby new potatoes.

*Try this:* MAIN MEAL: 144  PUDDING: 354

# Smoked Mackerel & Potato Salad

**SERVES 4**

½ tsp dry mustard powder
1 large egg yolk
salt and freshly ground
  black pepper
150 ml/¼ pint sunflower oil
1–2 tbsp lemon juice

450 g/1 lb baby
  new potatoes
25 g/1 oz butter
350 g/12 oz smoked
  mackerel fillets
4 celery stalks, trimmed and

finely chopped
3 tbsp creamed horseradish
150 ml/¼ pint crème fraîche
1 Little Gem lettuce, rinsed
  and roughly torn
8 cherry tomatoes, halved

Place the mustard powder and egg yolk in a small bowl with salt and pepper and whisk until blended. Add the oil, drop by drop, into the egg mixture, whisking continuously. When the mayonnaise is thick, add the lemon juice, drop by drop, until a smooth, glossy consistency is formed. Reserve.

Cook the potatoes in boiling salted water until tender, then drain. Cool slightly, then cut into halves or quarters, depending on size. Return to the saucepan and toss in the butter.

Remove the skin from the mackerel fillets and flake into pieces. Add to the potatoes in the saucepan, together with the celery.

Blend 4 tablespoons of the mayonnaise with the horseradish and crème fraîche. Season to taste with salt and pepper, then add to the potato and mackerel mixture and stir lightly.

Arrange the lettuce and tomatoes on four serving plates. Pile the smoked mackerel mixture on top of the lettuce, grind over a little pepper and serve with the remaining mayonnaise.

*Try this:* MAIN MEAL: 146   PUDDING: 360

# Chef's Rice Salad

**SERVES 4**

225 g/8 oz wild rice
½ cucumber
175 g/6 oz cherry tomatoes
6 spring onions, trimmed
5 tbsp extra-virgin olive oil
2 tbsp balsamic vinegar
1 tsp Dijon mustard

1 tsp caster sugar
salt and freshly ground
    black pepper
125 g/4 oz rocket
125 g/4 oz back bacon
125 g/4 oz cooked chicken
    meat, finely diced

125 g/4 oz Emmenthal
    cheese, grated
125 g/4 oz large cooked
    prawns, peeled
1 avocado, stoned, peeled
    and sliced, to garnish
warm crusty bread, to serve

Put the rice in in a saucepan of water and bring to the boil, stirring once or twice. Reduce the heat, cover and simmer gently for 30–50 minutes, depending on the texture you prefer. Drain well and reserve.

Thinly peel the cucumber, cut in half, then using a teaspoon, remove the seeds. Cut the cucumber into thin slices. Cut the tomatoes in quarters. Cut the spring onions into diagonal slices.

Whisk the olive oil with the vinegar, then whisk in the mustard and sugar. Season to taste with salt and pepper.

In a large bowl, gently toss together the cooled rice with the tomatoes, cucumber, spring onions and the rocket. Pour over the dressing and toss lightly together.

Heat a griddle pan and when hot cook the bacon on both sides for 4–6 minutes, or until crisp. Remove and chop. Arrange the prepared rocket salad on a platter, then arrange the bacon, chicken, cheese and prawns on top. Toss, if wished. Garnish with avocado slices and serve with plenty of warm, crusty bread.

*Try this:* MAIN MEAL: 142  PUDDING: 356

# Supreme Baked Potatoes

**SERVES 4**

4 large baking potatoes
40 g/1½ oz butter
1 tbsp sunflower oil
1 carrot, peeled
   and chopped

2 celery stalks, trimmed and
   finely chopped
200 g can white crab meat
2 spring onions, trimmed
   and finely chopped

salt and freshly ground
   black pepper
50 g/2 oz Cheddar
   cheese, grated
tomato salad, to serve

Preheat the oven to 200°C/400°F/Gas Mark 6. Scrub the potatoes and prick all over with a fork, or thread two potatoes onto two long metal skewers. Place the potatoes in the preheated oven for 1–1½ hours, or until soft to the touch. Allow to cool a little, then cut in half.

Scoop out the cooked potato and turn into a bowl, leaving a reasonably firm potato shell. Mash the cooked potato flesh, then mix in the butter and mash until the butter has melted.

While the potatoes are cooking, heat the oil in a frying pan and cook the carrot and celery for 2 minutes. Cover the pan tightly and continue to cook for another 5 minutes, or until the vegetables are tender.

Add the cooked vegetables to the bowl of mashed potato and mix well. Fold in the crab meat and the spring onions, then season to taste with salt and pepper.

Pile the mixture back into the potato shells and press in firmly. Sprinkle the grated cheese over the top and return the potato halves to the oven for 12–15 minutes until hot, golden and bubbling. Serve immediately with a tomato salad.

*Try this:* MAIN MEAL: 150  PUDDING: 360

# Special Rosti

**SERVES 4**

700 g/1½ lb potatoes,
    scrubbed but not peeled
salt and freshly ground
    black pepper
75 g/3 oz butter
1 large onion, peeled and
    finely chopped

1 garlic clove, peeled
    and crushed
2 tbsp freshly
    chopped parsley
1 tbsp olive oil
75 g/3 oz Parma ham,
    thinly sliced

50 g/2 oz sun-dried
    tomatoes, chopped
175 g/ 6 oz Emmenthal
    cheese, grated
mixed green salad,
    to serve

Cook the potatoes in a large saucepan of salted boiling water for about 10 minutes, until just tender. Drain in a colander, then rinse in cold water. Drain again. Leave until cool enough to handle, then peel off the skins.

Melt the butter in a large frying pan and gently fry the onion and garlic for about 3 minutes until softened and beginning to colour. Remove from the heat.

Coarsely grate the potatoes into a large bowl, then stir in the onion and garlic mixture. Sprinkle over the parsley and stir well to mix. Season to taste with salt and pepper.

Heat the oil in the frying pan and cover the base of the pan with half the potato mixture. Lay the slices of Parma ham on top. Sprinkle with the chopped sun-dried tomatoes, then scatter the grated Emmenthal over the top.

Finally, top with the remaining potato mixture. Cook over a low heat, pressing down with a palette knife from time to time, for 10–15 minutes, or until the bottom is golden brown. Carefully invert the rosti onto a large plate, then carefully slide back into the pan and cook the other side until golden. Serve cut into wedges with a mixed green salad.

*Try this:* MAIN MEAL: 154  PUDDING: 362

# Potato Skins

**SERVES 4**

4 large baking potatoes
2 tbsp olive oil
2 tsp paprika
125 g/4 oz pancetta,
    roughly chopped

6 tbsp double cream
125 g/4 oz Gorgonzola
    cheese
1 tbsp freshly
    chopped parsley

To serve:
reduced-calorie mayonnaise
sweet chilli dipping sauce
tossed green salad

Preheat the oven to 200°C/400°F/Gas Mark 6. Scrub the potatoes, then prick a few times with a fork or skewer and place directly on the top shelf of the oven. Bake in the preheated oven for at least 1 hour, or until tender. The potatoes are cooked when they yield gently to the pressure of your hand.

Set the potatoes aside until cool enough to handle, then cut in half and scoop the flesh into a bowl and reserve. Preheat the grill and line the grill rack with tinfoil.

Mix together the oil and the paprika and use half to brush the outside of the potato skins. Place on the grill rack under the preheated hot grill and cook for 5 minutes, or until crisp, turning as necessary.

Heat the remaining paprika-flavoured oil and gently fry the pancetta until crisp. Add to the potato flesh along with the cream, Gorgonzola cheese and parsley. Halve the potato skins and fill with the Gorgonzola filling. Return to the oven for a further 15 minutes to heat through. Sprinkle with a little more paprika and serve immediately with mayonnaise, sweet chilli sauce and a green salad.

*Try this:* MAIN MEAL: 174  PUDDING: 378

# Spicy Chicken Skewers with Mango Tabbouleh

**SERVES 4**

400 g/14 oz chicken
breast fillet
200 ml/7 fl oz natural
low fat yogurt
1 garlic clove, peeled
and crushed
1 small red chilli, deseeded
and finely chopped
½ tsp ground turmeric
finely grated rind and juice

of ½ lemon
sprigs of fresh mint,
to garnish

For the mango tabbouleh:
175 g/6 oz bulgur wheat
1 tsp olive oil
juice of ½ lemon
½ red onion, finely chopped
1 ripe mango, halved,

stoned, peeled
and chopped
¼ cucumber, finely diced
2 tbsp freshly
chopped parsley
2 tbsp freshly shredded mint
salt and finely ground
black pepper

If using wooden skewers, pre-soak them in cold water for at least 30 minutes. This stops them from burning during grilling.

Cut the chicken into 5 x 1 cm/2 x ½ inch strips and place in a shallow dish. Mix together the yogurt, garlic, chilli, turmeric, lemon rind and juice. Pour over the chicken and toss to coat. Cover and leave to marinate in the refrigerator for up to 8 hours.

To make the tabbouleh, put the bulgur wheat in a bowl. Pour over enough boiling water to cover. Put a plate over the bowl. Leave to soak for 20 minutes. Whisk together the oil and lemon juice in a bowl. Add the red onion and leave to marinade for 10 minutes. Drain the bulgur wheat and squeeze out any excess moisture in a clean tea towel. Add to the red onion with the mango, cucumber, herbs and season to taste with salt and pepper. Toss together.

Thread the chicken strips on to 8 wooden or metal skewers. Cook under a hot grill for 8 minutes. Turn and brush with the marinade, until the chicken is lightly browned and cooked through. Spoon the tabbouleh on to individual plates. Arrange the chicken skewers on top and garnish with the sprigs of mint. Serve warm or cold.

*Try this:* MAIN MEAL: 146  PUDDING: 352

# Chicken & Summer Vegetable Risotto

**SERVES 4**

1 litre/1¾ pint chicken or
    vegetable stock
225 g/8 oz baby
    asparagus spears
125 g/4 oz French beans
15 g/½ oz butter
1 small onion, peeled

and finely chopped
150 ml/¼ pint dry
    white wine
275 g/10 oz arborio rice
pinch of saffron strands
75 g/3 oz frozen
    peas, thawed

225 g/8 oz cooked chicken,
    skinned and diced
juice of ½ lemon
salt and freshly ground
    black pepper
25 g/1 oz Parmesan,
    shaved

Bring the stock to the boil in a large saucepan. Trim the asparagus and cut into 4 cm/1½ inch lengths. Blanch the asparagus in the stock for 1–2 minutes or until tender, then remove with a slotted spoon and reserve. Halve the green beans and cook in the boiling stock for 4 minutes. Remove and reserve. Turn down the heat and keep the stock barely simmering.

Melt the butter in a heavy-based saucepan. Add the onion and cook gently for about 5 minutes. Pour the wine into the pan and boil rapidly until the liquid has almost reduced. Add the rice and cook, stirring for 1 minute until the grains are coated and look translucent. Add the saffron and a ladle of the stock. Simmer, stirring all the time, until the stock has absorbed. Continue adding the stock, a ladle at a time, until it has all been absorbed.

After 15 minutes the risotto should be creamy with a slight bite to it. If not add a little more stock and cook for a few more minutes, or until it is of the correct texture and consistency. Add the peas, reserved vegetables, chicken and lemon juice. Season to taste with salt and pepper and cook for 3–4 minutes or until the chicken is thoroughly heated and piping hot.

Spoon the risotto on to warmed serving plates. Scatter each portion with a few shavings of Parmesan cheese and serve immediately.

*Try this:* MAIN MEAL: 186  PUDDING: 360

# Chicken & New Potatoes on Rosemary Skewers

**SERVES 4**

8 thick fresh rosemary
stems, at least 23 cm/
9 inches long
3–4 tbsp extra-virgin olive oil
2 garlic cloves, peeled
and crushed
1 tsp freshly chopped thyme
grated rind and juice

of 1 lemon
salt and freshly ground
black pepper
4 skinless chicken
breast fillets
16 small new potatoes,
peeled or scrubbed
8 very small onions or

shallots, peeled
1 large yellow or red
pepper, deseeded
lemon wedges, to garnish
parsley-flavoured cooked
rice, to serve

Preheat the grill and line the grill rack with tinfoil just before cooking. If using a barbecue, light at least 20 minutes before required. Strip the leaves from the rosemary stems, leaving about 5 cm/2 inches of soft leaves at the top. Chop the leaves coarsely and reserve. Using a sharp knife, cut the thicker woody ends of the stems to a point which can pierce the chicken pieces and potatoes. Blend the chopped rosemary, oil, garlic, thyme and lemon rind and juice in a shallow dish. Season to taste with salt and pepper. Cut the chicken into 4 cm/½ inch cubes, add to the flavoured oil and stir well. Cover, refrigerate for at least 30 minutes, turning occasionally.

Cook the potatoes in lightly salted boiling water for 10–12 minutes until just tender. Add the onions to the potatoes 2 minutes before the end of the cooking time. Drain, rinse under cold running water and leave to cool. Cut the pepper into 2.5 cm/1 inch squares.

Beginning with a piece of chicken and starting with the pointed end of the skewer, alternately thread equal amounts of chicken, potato, pepper and onion onto each rosemary skewer. Cover the leafy ends of the skewers with tinfoil to stop them from burning. Do not thread the chicken and vegetables too closely together on the skewer or the chicken may not cook completely. Cook the kebabs for 15 minutes, or until tender and golden, turning and brushing with either extra oil or the marinade. Remove the tinfoil, garnish with lemon wedges and serve on rice.

*Try this:* MAIN MEAL: 160  PUDDING: 362

# Warm Chicken & Potato Salad with Peas & Mint

**SERVES 4-6**

450 g/1 lb new potatoes, peeled or scrubbed and cut into bite-sized pieces
salt and freshly ground black pepper
2 tbsp cider vinegar
175 g/6 oz frozen garden peas, thawed

1 small ripe avocado
4 cooked chicken breasts, about 450 g/1 lb in weight, skinned and diced
2 tbsp freshly chopped mint
2 heads Little Gem lettuce
fresh mint sprigs, to garnish

For the dressing:
2 tbsp raspberry or sherry vinegar
2 tsp Dijon mustard
1 tsp clear honey
50 ml/2 fl oz sunflower oil
50 ml/2 fl oz extra virgin olive oil

Cook the potatoes in lightly salted boiling water for 15 minutes, or until just tender when pierced with the tip of a sharp knife; do not overcook. Rinse under cold running water to cool slightly, then drain and turn into a large bowl. Sprinkle with the cider vinegar and toss gently.

Run the peas under hot water to ensure that they are thawed, pat dry with absorbent kitchen paper and add to the potatoes.

Cut the avocado in half lengthways and remove the stone. Peel and cut the avocado into cubes and add to the potatoes and peas. Add the chicken and stir together lightly.

To make the dressing, place all the ingredients in a screw-top jar, with a little salt and pepper and shake well to mix; add a little more oil if the flavour is too sharp. Pour over the salad and toss gently to coat. Sprinkle in half the mint and stir lightly.

Separate the lettuce leaves and spread onto a large shallow serving plate. Spoon the salad on top and sprinkle with the remaining mint. Garnish with mint sprigs and serve.

*Try this:* MAIN MEAL: 178   PUDDING: 380

# Warm Fruity Rice Salad

**SERVES 4**

175 g/6 oz mixed basmati
and wild rice
125 g/4 oz skinless
chicken breast
300 ml/½ pint chicken
or vegetable stock
125 g/4 oz ready-to-eat
dried apricots

125 g/4 oz ready-to-eat
dried dates
3 sticks celery

For the dressing:
2 tbsp sunflower oil
1 tbsp white wine vinegar
4 tbsp lemon juice

1–2 tsp clear honey, warmed
1 tsp Dijon mustard
freshly ground black pepper

To garnish:
6 spring onions
sprigs of fresh coriander

Place the rice in a pan of boiling salted water and cook for 15–20 minutes or until tender. Rinse thoroughly with boiling water and reserve.

Meanwhile wipe the chicken and place in a shallow saucepan with the stock.

Bring to the boil, cover and simmer for about 15 minutes or until the chicken is cooked thoroughly and the juices run clear.

Leave the chicken in the stock until cool enough to handle, then cut into thin slices.

Chop the apricots and dates into small pieces. Peel any tough membranes from the outside of the celery and chop into dice. Fold the apricots, dates, celery and sliced chicken into the warm rice.

Make the dressing by whisking all the ingredients together in a small bowl until mixed thoroughly. Pour 2–3 tablespoons over the rice and stir in gently and evenly. Serve the remaining dressing separately.

Trim and chop the spring onions. Sprinkle the spring onions over the top of the salad and garnish with the sprigs of coriander. Serve while still warm.

*Try this:* MAIN MEAL: 148  PUDDING: 358

# Sweet & Sour Rice with Chicken

**SERVES 4**

| | | |
|---|---|---|
| 4 spring onions | 1 garlic clove, peeled | 4 tbsp tomato ketchup |
| 2 tsp sesame oil | and crushed | 1 tbsp tomato purée |
| 1 tsp Chinese five- | 1 medium onion, peeled and | 2 tbsp honey |
| spice powder | sliced into thin wedges | 1 tbsp vinegar |
| 450 g/1 lb chicken breast, | 225 g/8 oz long-grain | 1 tbsp dark soy sauce |
| cut into cubes | white rice | 1 carrot, peeled and cut |
| 1 tbsp oil | 600 ml/1 pint water | into matchsticks |

Trim the spring onions, then cut lengthways into fine strips. Drop into a large bowl of iced water and reserve.

Mix together the sesame oil and Chinese five-spice powder and use to rub into the cubed chicken. Heat the wok, then add the oil and when hot, cook the garlic and onion for 2–3 minutes, or until transparent and softened.

Add the chicken and stir-fry over a medium-high heat until the chicken is golden and cooked through. Using a slotted spoon, remove from the wok and keep warm.

Stir the rice into the wok and add the water, tomato ketchup, tomato purée, honey, vinegar and soy sauce. Stir well to mix. Bring to the boil, then simmer until almost all of the liquid is absorbed. Stir in the carrot and reserved chicken and continue to cook for 3–4 minutes.

Drain the spring onions, which will have become curly. Garnish with the spring onion curls and serve immediately with the rice and chicken.

*Try this:* MAIN MEAL: 144  PUDDING: 370

# Rice & Papaya Salad

**SERVES 4**

175 g/6 oz easy-cook
  basmati rice
1 cinnamon stick, bruised
1 bird's-eye chilli, deseeded
  and finely chopped
rind and juice of 2 limes
rind and juice of 2 lemons
2 tbsp Thai fish sauce

1 tbsp soft light brown sugar
1 papaya, peeled and
  seeds removed
1 mango, peeled and
  stone removed
1 green chilli, deseeded and
  finely chopped
2 tbsp freshly chopped

  coriander
1 tbsp freshly chopped mint
250 g/9 oz cooked chicken
50 g/2 oz roasted
  peanuts, chopped
strips of pitta bread, to serve

Rinse and drain the rice and pour into a saucepan. Add 450 ml/¾ pint boiling salted water and the cinnamon stick. Bring to the boil, reduce the heat to a very low heat, cover and cook without stirring for 15–18 minutes, or until all the liquid is absorbed. The rice should be light and fluffy and have steam holes on the surface. Remove the cinnamon stick and stir in the rind from 1 lime.

To make the dressing, place the bird's-eye chilli, remaining rind and lime and lemon juice, fish sauce and sugar in a food processor, mix for a few minutes until blended. Alternatively, place all these ingredients in a screw-top jar and shake until well blended. Pour half the dressing over the hot rice and toss until the rice glistens.

Slice the papaya and mango into thin slices, then place in a bowl. Add the chopped green chilli, coriander and mint. Place the chicken on a chopping board, then remove and discard any skin or sinews. Cut into fine shreds and add to the bowl with the chopped peanuts.

Add the remaining dressing to the chicken mixture and stir until all the ingredients are lightly coated. Spoon the rice onto a platter, pile the chicken mixture on top and serve with warm strips of pitta bread.

*Try this:* MAIN MEAL: 152  PUDDING: 352

# Courgette & Tarragon Tortilla

**SERVES 6**

700 g/1½ lb potatoes
3 tbsp olive oil
1 onion, peeled and
   thinly sliced

salt and freshly ground
   black pepper
1 courgette, trimmed and
   thinly sliced

6 medium eggs
2 tbsp freshly chopped
   tarragon
tomato wedges, to serve

Peel the potatoes and thinly slice. Dry the slices in a clean tea towel to get them as dry as possible. Heat the oil in a large heavy-based pan, add the onion and cook for 3 minutes. Add the potatoes with a little salt and pepper, then stir the potatoes and onion lightly to coat in the oil.

Reduce the heat to the lowest possible setting, cover and cook gently for 5 minutes. Turn the potatoes and onion over and continue to cook for a further 5 minutes. Give the pan a shake every now and again to ensure that the potatoes do not stick to the base or burn. Add the courgette, then cover and cook for a further 10 minutes.

Beat the eggs and tarragon together and season to taste with salt and pepper. Pour the egg mixture over the vegetables and return to the heat. Cook on a low heat for up to 20–25 minutes, or until there is no liquid egg left on the surface of the tortilla.

Turn the tortilla over by inverting the tortilla onto the lid or onto a flat plate. Return the pan to the heat and cook for a final 3–5 minutes, or until the underside is golden brown. If preferred, place the tortilla under a preheated grill for 4 minutes, or until set and golden brown on top. Cut into small squares and serve hot or cold with tomato wedges.

*Try this:* MAIN MEAL: 168   PUDDING: 380

# Indonesian Salad with Peanut Dressing

**SERVES 4**

225 g/8 oz new potatoes, scrubbed
1 large carrot, peeled and cut into matchsticks
125 g/4 oz French beans, trimmed
225 g/8 oz tiny cauliflower florets
125 g/4 oz cucumber, cut into matchsticks
75 g/3 oz fresh bean sprouts
3 medium eggs, hard-boiled and quartered

For the peanut dressing:
2 tbsp sesame oil
1 garlic clove, peeled and crushed
1 red chilli, deseeded and finely chopped
150 g/5 oz crunchy peanut butter
6 tbsp hot vegetable stock
2 tsp soft light brown sugar
2 tsp dark soy sauce
1 tbsp lime juice

Cook the potatoes in a saucepan of boiling salted water for 15–20 minutes until tender. Remove with a slotted spoon and thickly slice into a large bowl. Keep the saucepan of water boiling.

Add the carrot, French beans and cauliflower to the water, return to the boil and cook for 2 minutes, or until just tender. Drain and refresh under cold running water, then drain well. Add to the potatoes with the cucumber and bean sprouts.

To make the dressing, gently heat the sesame oil in a small saucepan. Add the garlic and chilli and cook for a few seconds, then remove from the heat. Stir in the peanut butter.

Stir in the stock, a little at a time. Add the remaining ingredients and mix together to make a thick, creamy dressing.

Divide the vegetables between four plates and arrange the eggs on top. Drizzle the dressing over the salad and serve immediately.

*Try this:* MAIN MEAL: 190   PUDDING: 360

# Wild Mushroom Risotto

**SERVES 4**

15 g/½ oz dried porcini
1.1 litres/2 pints
   vegetable stock
75 g/3 oz butter
1 tbsp olive oil
1 onion, peeled and chopped
2–4 garlic cloves, peeled
   and chopped
1–2 red chillies, deseeded

and chopped
225 g/8 oz wild mushrooms,
   wiped and halved, if large
125 g/4 oz button
   mushrooms, wiped
   and sliced
350 g/12 oz Arborio rice
175 g/6 oz large cooked
   prawns, peeled

150 ml/¼ pint white wine
salt and freshly ground
   black pepper
1 tbsp lemon zest
1 tbsp freshly snipped chives
2 tbsp freshly
   chopped parsley

Soak the porcini in 300 ml/½ pint of very hot, but not boiling water for 30 minutes. Drain, reserving the mushrooms and soaking liquid. Pour the stock into a saucepan, and bring to the boil, then reduce the heat to keep it simmering.

Melt the butter and oil in a large deep frying pan, add the onion, garlic and chillies and cook gently for 5 minutes. Add the wild and button mushrooms with the drained porcini, and continue to cook for 4–5 minutes, stirring frequently.

Stir in the rice and cook for 1 minute. Strain the reserved soaking liquid and stir into the rice with a little of the hot stock. Cook gently, stirring frequently, until the liquid is absorbed. Continue to add most of the stock, a ladleful at a time, cooking after each addition, until the rice is tender and the risotto looks creamy.

Add the prawns and wine along with the last additions of stock. When the prawns are hot and all the liquid is absorbed, season to taste with salt and pepper. Remove from the heat and stir in the lemon zest, chives and parsley, reserving some for the garnish. Garnish and serve.

*Try this:* MAIN MEAL: 142 PUDDING: 378

# Warm Potato, Pear & Pecan Salad

**SERVES 4**

900 g/2 lb new potatoes,
    preferably red-skinned,
    unpeeled
salt and freshly ground
    black pepper

1 tsp Dijon mustard
2 tsp white wine vinegar
3 tbsp groundnut oil
1 tbsp hazelnut or walnut oil
2 tsp poppy seeds

2 firm ripe dessert pears
2 tsp lemon juice
175 g/6 oz baby
    spinach leaves
75 g/3 oz toasted pecan nuts

Scrub the potatoes, then cook in a saucepan of lightly salted boiling water for 15 minutes, or until tender. Drain, cut into halves, or quarters if large, and place in a serving bowl.

In a small bowl or jug, whisk together the mustard and vinegar. Gradually add the oils until the mixture begins to thicken. Stir in the poppy seeds and season to taste with salt and pepper.

Pour about two-thirds of the dressing over the hot potatoes and toss gently to coat. Leave until the potatoes have soaked up the dressing and are just warm.

Meanwhile, quarter and core the pears. Cut into thin slices, then sprinkle with the lemon juice to prevent them from going brown. Add to the potatoes with the spinach leaves and toasted pecan nuts. Gently mix together.

Drizzle the remaining dressing over the salad. Serve immediately before the spinach starts to wilt.

*Try this:* MAIN MEAL: 188  PUDDING: 352

# Mediterranean Potato Salad

**SERVES 4**

700 g/1½ lb small waxy potatoes
2 red onions, peeled and roughly chopped
1 yellow pepper, deseeded and roughly chopped
1 green pepper, deseeded and roughly chopped

6 tbsp extra-virgin olive oil
125 g/4 oz ripe tomatoes, chopped
50 g/2 oz pitted black olives, sliced
125 g/4 oz feta cheese
3 tbsp freshly chopped parsley

2 tbsp white wine vinegar
1 tsp Dijon mustard
1 tsp clear honey
salt and freshly ground black pepper
sprigs of fresh parsley, to garnish

Preheat the oven to 200°C/400°F/Gas Mark 6. Place the potatoes in a large saucepan of salted water, bring to the boil and simmer until just tender. Do not overcook. Drain and plunge into cold water, to stop them from cooking further.

Place the onions in a bowl with the yellow and green peppers, then pour over 2 tablespoons of the olive oil. Stir and spoon onto a large baking tray. Cook in the preheated oven for 25–30 minutes, or until the vegetables are tender and lightly charred in places, stirring occasionally. Remove from the oven and transfer to a large bowl.

Cut the potatoes into bite-sized pieces and mix with the roasted onions and peppers. Add the tomatoes and olives to the potatoes. Crumble over the feta cheese and sprinkle with the chopped parsley.

Whisk together the remaining olive oil, vinegar, mustard and honey, then season to taste with salt and pepper. Pour the dressing over the potatoes and toss gently together. Garnish with parsley sprigs and serve immediately.

*Try this:* MAIN MEAL: 200  PUDDING: 364

# Peperonata

**SERVES 6**

2 red peppers
2 yellow peppers
450 g/1 lb waxy potatoes
1 large onion
2 tbsp good-quality virgin
   olive oil

700 g/1½ lb tomatoes,
   peeled, deseeded
   and chopped
2 small courgettes
50 g/2 oz pitted black
   olives, quartered

small handful basil leaves
salt and freshly ground
   black pepper
crusty bread, to serve

Prepare the peppers by halving them lengthwise and removing the stems, seeds and membranes.

Cut the peppers lengthwise into strips about 1 cm/½ inch wide. Peel the potatoes and cut into rough dice, about 2.5–3 cm/1–1¼ inch across. Cut the onion lengthwise into 8 wedges.

Heat the olive oil in a large saucepan over a medium heat.

Add the onion and cook for about 5 minutes, or until starting to brown.

Add the peppers, potatoes, tomatoes, courgettes, black olives and about four torn basil leaves. Season to taste with salt and pepper.

Stir the mixture, cover and cook over a very low heat for about 40 minutes, or until the vegetables are tender but still hold their shape. Garnish with the remaining basil. Transfer to a serving bowl and serve immediately, with chunks of crusty bread.

*Try this:* MAIN MEAL: 162  PUDDING: 374

# Mediterranean Rice Salad

**SERVES 4**

250 g/9 oz Camargue red rice
2 sun-dried tomatoes, finely chopped
2 garlic cloves, peeled and finely chopped
4 tbsp oil from a jar of sun-dried tomatoes
2 tsp balsamic vinegar

2 tsp red wine vinegar
salt and freshly ground black pepper
1 red onion, peeled and thinly sliced
1 yellow pepper, quartered and deseeded
1 red pepper, quartered

and deseeded
½ cucumber, peeled and diced
6 ripe plum tomatoes, cut into wedges
1 fennel bulb, halved and thinly sliced
fresh basil leaves, to garnish

Cook the rice in a saucepan of lightly salted boiling water for 35–40 minutes, or until tender. Drain well and reserve.

Whisk the sun-dried tomatoes, garlic, oil and vinegars together in a small bowl or jug. Season to taste with salt and pepper. Put the red onion in a large bowl, pour over the dressing and leave to allow the flavours to develop.

Put the peppers, skin-side up on a grill rack and cook under a preheated hot grill for 5–6 minutes, or until blackened and charred. Remove and place in a plastic bag. When cool enough to handle, peel off the skins and slice the peppers.

Add the peppers, cucumber, tomatoes, fennel and rice to the onions. Mix gently together to coat in the dressing. Cover and chill in the refrigerator for 30 minutes to allow the flavours to mingle.

Remove the salad from the refrigerator and leave to stand at room temperature for 20 minutes. Garnish with fresh basil leaves and serve.

*Try this:* MAIN MEAL: 142   PUDDING: 366

# Main Meals

# Gingered Cod Steaks

**SERVES 4**

2.5 cm /1 inch piece
  fresh root ginger, peeled
4 spring onions
2 tsp freshly
  chopped parsley

1 tbsp soft brown sugar
4 x 175 g /6 oz thick
  cod steaks
salt and freshly ground
  black pepper

25 g/1 oz half-fat butter
freshly cooked vegetables,
  to serve

Preheat the grill and line the grill rack with a layer of tinfoil. Coarsely grate the piece of ginger. Trim the spring onions and cut into thin strips.

Mix the spring onions, ginger, chopped parsley and sugar. Add 1 tablespoon of water.

Wipe the fish steaks. Season to taste with salt and pepper. Place on to four separate 20.5 x 20.5 cm/8 x 8 inch tinfoil squares.

Carefully spoon the spring onions and ginger mixture over the fish.

Cut the butter into small cubes and place over the fish.

Loosely fold the foil over the steaks to enclose the fish and to make a parcel.

Place under the preheated grill and cook for 10–12 minutes or until cooked and the flesh has turned opaque.

Place the fish parcels on individual serving plates. Serve immediately with the freshly cooked vegetables.

*Try this:* FOR STARTERS: 32  FOR PUDDING: 360

# Ratatouille Mackerel

**SERVES 4**

1 red pepper
1 tbsp olive oil
1 red onion, peeled
1 garlic clove, peeled and
    thinly sliced
2 courgettes, trimmed and

cut into thick slices
400 g can chopped tomatoes
sea salt and freshly ground
    black pepper
4 x 275 g/10 oz small
    mackerel, cleaned and

heads removed
spray of olive oil
lemon juice for drizzling
12 fresh basil leaves
couscous or rice mixed with
    chopped parsley, to serve

Preheat the oven to 190°C/375°F/Gas Mark 5. Cut the top off the red pepper, remove the seeds and membrane, then cut into chunks. Cut the red onion into thick wedges.

Heat the oil in a large pan and cook the onion and garlic for 5 minutes or until beginning to soften.

Add the pepper chunks and courgettes slices and cook for a further 5 minutes.

Pour in the chopped tomatoes with their juice and cook for a further 5 minutes. Season to taste with salt and pepper and pour into an ovenproof dish.

Season the fish with salt and pepper and arrange on top of the vegetables. Spray with a little olive oil and lemon juice. Cover and cook in the preheated oven for 20 minutes.

Remove the cover, add the basil leaves and return to the oven for a further 5 minutes. Serve immediately with couscous or rice mixed with parsley.

# Haddock with an Olive Crust

**SERVES 4**

12 pitted black olives,
  finely chopped
75 g/3 oz fresh white
  breadcrumbs
1 tbsp freshly
  chopped tarragon
1 garlic clove, peeled

  and crushed
3 spring onions, trimmed
  and finely chopped
1 tbsp olive oil
4 x 175 g/6 oz thick skinless
  haddock fillets

To serve:
freshly cooked carrots
freshly cooked beans

Preheat the oven to 190°C/375°F/Gas Mark 5. Place the black olives in a small bowl with the breadcrumbs and add the chopped tarragon.

Add the garlic to the olives with the chopped spring onions and the olive oil. Mix together lightly.

Wipe the fillets with either a clean damp cloth or damp kitchen paper, then place on a lightly oiled baking sheet.

Place spoonfuls of the olive and breadcrumb mixture on top of each fillet and press the mixture down lightly and evenly over the top of the fish.

Bake the fish in the preheated oven for 20–25 minutes or until the fish is cooked thoroughly and the topping is golden brown. Serve immediately with the freshly cooked carrots and beans.

*Try this:* FOR STARTERS: 18  FOR PUDDING: 362

# Hot Salsa–filled Sole

**SERVES 4**

8 x 175 g/6 oz lemon
   sole fillets, skinned
150 ml/¼ pint orange juice
2 tbsp lemon juice

For the salsa:
1 small mango

8 cherry tomatoes,
   quartered
1 small red onion, peeled
   and finely chopped
pinch of sugar
1 red chilli
2 tbsp rice vinegar

zest and juice of 1 lime
1 tbsp olive oil
sea salt and freshly ground
   black pepper
2 tbsp freshly chopped mint
lime wedges, to garnish
salad leaves, to serve

First make the salsa. Peel the mango and cut the flesh away from the stone. Chop finely and place in a small bowl. Add the cherry tomatoes to the mango together with the onion and sugar.

Cut the top of the chilli. Slit down the side and discard the seeds and the membrane (the skin to which the seeds are attached). Finely chop the chilli and add to the mango mixture with the vinegar, lime zest, juice and oil. Season to taste with salt and pepper. Mix thoroughly and leave to stand for 30 minutes to allow the flavours to develop.

Lay the fish fillets on a board skinned side up and pile the salsa on the tail end of the fillets. Fold the fillets in half, season and place in a large shallow frying pan. Pour over the orange and lemon juice.

Bring to a gentle boil, then reduce the heat to a simmer. Cover and cook on a low heat for 7–10 minutes, adding a little water if the liquid is evaporating. Remove the cover, add the mint and cook uncovered for a further 3 minutes. Garnish with lime wedges and serve immediately with the salad.

# Citrus–grilled Plaice

**SERVES 4**

1 tsp sunflower oil
1 onion, peeled
  and chopped
1 orange pepper, deseeded
  and chopped
175 g/6 oz long-grain rice
150 ml/¼ pint orange juice
2 tbsp lemon juice

225 ml/8 fl oz
  vegetable stock
spray of oil
4 x 175 g/6 oz plaice
  fillets, skinned
1 orange
1 lemon
25 g/1 oz half-fat butter or

low fat spread
2 tbsp freshly
  chopped tarragon
salt and freshly ground
  black pepper
lemon wedges,
  to garnish

Heat the oil in a large frying pan, then sauté the onion, pepper and rice for 2 minutes.

Add the orange and lemon juice and bring to the boil. Reduce the heat, add half the stock and simmer for 15–20 minutes, or until the rice is tender, adding the remaining stock as necessary.

Preheat the grill. Finely spray the base of the grill pan with oil. Place the plaice fillets in the base and reserve.

Finely grate the orange and lemon rind. Squeeze the juice from half of each fruit.

Melt the butter or low-fat spread in a small saucepan. Add the grated rind, juice and half of the tarragon and use to baste the plaice fillets.

Cook one side only of the fish under the preheated grill at a medium heat for 4–6 minutes, basting continuously.

Once the rice is cooked, stir in the remaining tarragon and season to taste with salt and pepper. Garnish the fish with the lemon wedges and serve immediately with the rice.

*Try this:* FOR STARTERS: 24  FOR PUDDING: 361

# Fish Lasagne

**SERVES 4**

75 g/3 oz mushrooms
1 tsp sunflower oil
1 small onion, peeled and
  finely chopped
1 tbsp freshly
  chopped oregano
400 g can chopped tomatoes
1 tbsp tomato purée
salt and freshly ground

black pepper
450 g/1 lb cod or haddock
  fillets, skinned
9–12 sheets pre-cooked
  lasagne verde

For the topping:
1 medium egg, beaten
125 g/4 oz cottage cheese

150 ml/¼ pint low-fat
  natural yogurt
50 g/2 oz half-fat Cheddar
  cheese, grated

To serve:
mixed salad leaves
cherry tomatoes

Preheat the oven to 190°C/375°F/Gas Mark 5. Wipe the mushrooms, trim the stalks and chop. Heat the oil in a large heavy-based pan, add the onion and gently cook the onion for 3–5 minutes or until soft.

Stir in the mushrooms, the oregano and the chopped tomatoes with their juice. Blend the tomato purée with 1 tablespoon of water. Stir into the pan and season to taste with salt and pepper. Bring the sauce to the boil, then simmer uncovered for 5–10 minutes.

Remove as many of the tiny pin bones as possible from the fish and cut into cubes and add to the tomato sauce mixture. Stir gently and remove the pan from the heat.

Cover the base of an ovenproof dish with 2–3 sheets of the lasagne verde. Top with half of the fish mixture. Repeat the layers finishing with the lasagne sheets.

To make the topping, mix together the beaten egg, cottage cheese and yogurt. Pour over the lasagne and sprinkle with the cheese. Cook the lasagne in the preheated oven for 40–45 minutes or until the topping is golden brown and bubbling. Serve the lasagne immediately with the mixed salad leaves and cherry tomatoes.

*Try this:* FOR STARTERS: 22   FOR PUDDING: 366

# Zesty Whole–baked Fish

**SERVES 8**

1.8 kg/4 lb whole
   salmon, cleaned
sea salt and freshly ground
   black pepper
50 g/2 oz low-fat spread
1 garlic clove, peeled
   and finely sliced

zest and juice of 1 lemon
zest of 1 orange
1 tsp freshly grated nutmeg
3 tbsp Dijon mustard
2 tbsp fresh
   white breadcrumbs
2 bunches fresh dill

1 bunch fresh tarragon
1 lime sliced
150 ml/¼ pint half-fat
   crème fraîche
450 ml/¾ pint fromage frais
dill sprigs,
   to garnish

Preheat the oven to 220°C/425°F/Gas Mark 7. Lightly rinse the fish and pat dry with absorbent kitchen paper. Season the cavity with a little salt and pepper. Make several diagonal cuts across the flesh of the fish and season.

Mix together the low-fat spread, garlic, lemon and orange zest and juice, nutmeg, mustard and fresh breadcrumbs. Mix well together. Spoon the breadcrumb mixture into the slits with a small sprig of dill. Place the remaining herbs inside the fish cavity. Weigh the fish and calculate the cooking time. Allow 10 minutes per 450 g/1 lb.

Lay the fish on a double thickness tinfoil. If liked, smear the fish with a little low fat spread. Top with the lime slices and fold the foil into a parcel. Chill in the refrigerator for about 15 minutes.

Place in a roasting tin and cook in the preheated oven for the calculated cooking time. Fifteen minutes before the end of cooking, open the foil and return until the skin begins to crisp. Remove the fish from the oven and stand for 10 minutes.

Pour the juices from the roasting tin into a saucepan. Bring to the boil and stir in the crème fraîche and fromage frais. Simmer for 3 minutes or until hot. Garnish with dill sprigs and serve immediately.

*Try this:* FOR STARTERS: 46   FOR PUDDING: 354

# Traditional Fish Pie

**SERVES 4**

450 g/1 lb cod or coley fillets, skinned
450 ml/¾ pint milk
1 small onion, peeled and quartered
salt and freshly ground black pepper

900 g/2 lb potatoes, peeled and cut into chunks
100 g/3½ oz butter
125 g/4 oz large prawns
2 large eggs, hard-boiled and quartered
198 g can of

sweetcorn, drained
2 tbsp freshly chopped parsley
3 tbsp plain flour
50 g/2 oz Cheddar cheese, grated

Preheat the oven to 200°C/400°F/Gas Mark 6, about 15 minutes before cooking. Place the fish in a shallow frying pan, pour over 300 ml/½ pint of the milk and add the onion. Season to taste with salt and pepper. Bring to the boil and simmer for 8–10 minutes until the fish is cooked. Remove the fish with a slotted spoon and place in a 1.4 litre/2½ pint baking dish. Strain the cooking liquid and reserve.

Boil the potatoes until soft, then mash with 40 g/1½ oz of the butter and 2–3 tablespoons of the remaining milk. Reserve.

Arrange the prawns and sliced eggs on top of the fish, then scatter over the sweetcorn and sprinkle with the parsley.

Melt the remaining butter in a saucepan, stir in the flour and cook gently for 1 minute, stirring. Whisk in the reserved cooking liquid and remaining milk. Cook for 2 minutes, or until thickened, then pour over the fish mixture and cool slightly.

Spread the mashed potato over the top of the pie and sprinkle over the grated cheese. Bake in the preheated over for 30 minutes until golden. Serve immediately.

*Try this:* FOR STARTERS: 42   FOR PUDDING: 352

# Tuna & Mushroom Ragout

**SERVES 4**

225 g/8 oz basmati and wild rice
50 g/2 oz butter
1 tbsp olive oil
1 large onion, peeled and finely chopped
1 garlic clove, peeled and crushed
300 g/11 oz baby button

mushrooms, wiped and halved
2 tbsp plain flour
400 g can chopped tomatoes
1 tbsp freshly chopped parsley
dash of Worcestershire sauce
400 g can tuna in oil, drained

salt and freshly ground black pepper
4 tbsp Parmesan cheese, grated
1 tbsp freshly shredded basil

To serve:
green salad
garlic bread

Cook the basmati and wild rice in a saucepan of boiling salted water for 20 minutes, then drain and return to the pan. Stir in half of the butter, cover the pan and leave to stand for 2 minutes until all of the butter has melted.

Heat the oil and the remaining butter in a frying pan and cook the onion for 1–2 minutes until soft. Add the garlic and mushrooms and continue to cook for a further 3 minutes.

Stir in the flour and cook for 1 minute, then add the tomatoes and bring the sauce to the boil. Add the parsley, Worcestershire sauce and tuna and simmer gently for 3 minutes. Season to taste with salt and freshly ground pepper.

Stir the rice well, then spoon onto 4 serving plates and top with the tuna and mushroom mixture. Sprinkle with a spoonful of grated Parmesan cheese and some shredded basil for each portion and serve immediately with a green salad and chunks of garlic bread.

*Try this:* FOR STARTERS: 30   FOR PUDDING: 356

# Coconut Fish Curry

**SERVES 4**

2 tbsp sunflower oil
1 medium onion, peeled and
  very finely chopped
1 yellow pepper, deseeded
  and finely chopped
1 garlic clove, peeled
  and crushed
1 tbsp mild curry paste
2.5 cm/1 inch piece of root
  ginger, peeled and grated
1 red chilli, deseeded and

finely chopped
400 ml can coconut milk
700 g/1½ lb firm white fish,
  e.g. monkfish fillets,
  skinned and cut
  into chunks
225 g/8 oz basmati rice
1 tbsp freshly
  chopped coriander
1 tbsp mango chutney
salt and freshly ground

black pepper

To garnish:
lime wedges
fresh coriander sprigs

To serve:
Greek yogurt
warm naan bread

Put 1 tablespoon of the oil into a large frying pan and cook the onion, pepper and garlic for 5 minutes, or until soft. Add the remaining oil, curry paste, ginger and chilli and cook for a further minute.

Pour in the coconut milk and bring to the boil, reduce the heat and simmer gently for 5 minutes, stirring occasionally. Add the monkfish to the pan and continue to simmer gently for 5–10 minutes, or until the fish is tender, but not overcooked.

Meanwhile, cook the rice in a saucepan of boiling salted water for 15 minutes, or until tender. Drain the rice thoroughly and turn out into a serving dish.

Stir the chopped coriander and chutney gently into the fish curry and season to taste with salt and pepper. Spoon the fish curry over the cooked rice, garnish with lime wedges and coriander sprigs and serve immediately with spoonfuls of Greek yogurt and warm naan bread.

*Try this:* FOR STARTERS: 50   FOR PUDDING: 362

# Russian Fish Pie

**SERVES 4-6**

450 g/1 lb orange roughly or haddock fillet
150 ml/¼ pint dry white wine
salt and freshly ground black pepper
75 g/3 oz butter or margarine
1 large onion, peeled and finely chopped

75 g/3 oz long-grain rice
1 tbsp freshly chopped dill
125 g/4 oz baby button mushrooms, quartered
125 g/4 oz peeled prawns, thawed if frozen
3 medium eggs, hard-boiled and chopped
550 g/1¼ lb ready-prepared

puff pastry, thawed if frozen
1 small egg, beaten with a pinch of salt
assorted bitter salad leaves, to serve

Preheat the oven to 200°C/400°F/Gas Mark 6, 15 minutes before cooking. Place the fish in a shallow frying pan with the wine, 150 ml/¼ pint water and salt and pepper. Simmer for 8–10 minutes. Strain the fish, reserving the liquid, and when cool enough to handle, flake into a bowl.

Melt the butter or margarine in a saucepan and cook the onions for 2–3 minutes, then add the rice, reserved fish liquid and dill. Season lightly. Cover and simmer for 10 minutes, then stir in the mushrooms and cook for a further 10 minutes, or until all the liquid is absorbed. Mix the rice with the cooked fish, prawns and eggs. Leave to cool.

Roll half the pastry out on a lightly floured surface into a 23 x 30.5 cm/9 x 12 inch rectangle. Place on a dampened baking sheet and arrange the fish mixture on top, leaving a 1 cm/½ inch border. Brush the border with a little water.

Roll out the remaining pastry to a rectangle and use to cover the fish. Brush the edges lightly with a little of the beaten egg and press to seal. Roll out the pastry trimmings and use to decorate the top. Chill in the refrigerator for 30 minutes. Brush with the beaten egg and bake for 30 minutes, or until golden. Serve immediately with salad leaves.

# Chunky Halibut Casserole

**SERVES 6**

50 g/2 oz butter
  or margarine
2 large onions, peeled and
  sliced into rings
1 red pepper, deseeded and
  roughly chopped
450 g/1 lb potatoes, peeled
450 g/1 lb courgettes,

trimmed and thickly sliced
2 tbsp plain flour
1 tbsp paprika
2 tsp vegetable oil
300 ml/½ pint white wine
150 ml/¼ pint fish stock
400 g can chopped tomatoes
2 tbsp freshly chopped basil

salt and freshly ground
  black pepper
450 g/1 lb halibut fillet,
  skinned and cut into
  2.5 cm/1 inch cubes
sprigs of fresh basil,
  to garnish
freshly cooked rice, to serve

Melt the butter or margarine in a large saucepan, add the onions and pepper and cook for 5 minutes, or until softened.

Cut the peeled potatoes into 2.5 cm/1 inch dice, rinse lightly and shake dry, then add them to the onions and pepper in the saucepan. Add the courgettes and cook, stirring frequently, for a further 2–3 minutes.

Sprinkle the flour, paprika and vegetable oil into the saucepan and cook, stirring continuously, for 1 minute. Pour in 150 ml/¼ pint of the wine, with all the stock and the chopped tomatoes, and bring to the boil.

Add the basil to the casserole, season to taste with salt and pepper and cover. Simmer for 15 minutes, then add the halibut and the remaining wine and simmer very gently for a further 5–7 minutes, or until the fish and vegetables are just tender. Garnish with basil sprigs and serve immediately with freshly cooked rice.

*Try this:* FOR STARTERS: 36  FOR PUDDING: 372

# Cheesy Vegetable & Prawn Bake

**SERVES 4**

175 g/6 oz long-grain rice
salt and freshly ground
black pepper
1 garlic clove, peeled
and crushed
1 large egg, beaten
3 tbsp freshly shredded basil

4 tbsp Parmesan
cheese, grated
125 g/4 oz baby asparagus
spears, trimmed
150 g/5 oz baby
carrots, trimmed
150 g/5 oz fine green

beans, trimmed
150 g/5 oz cherry tomatoes
175 g/6 oz peeled prawns,
thawed if frozen
125 g/4 oz mozzarella
cheese, thinly sliced

Preheat the oven to 200°C/400°F/Gas Mark 6, about 10 minutes before required. Cook the rice in lightly salted boiling water for 12–15 minutes, or until tender, drain. Stir in the garlic, beaten egg, shredded basil, 2 tablespoons of the Parmesan cheese and season to taste with salt and pepper. Press this mixture into a greased 23 cm/9 inch square ovenproof dish and reserve.

Bring a large saucepan of water to the boil, then drop in the asparagus, carrots and green beans. Return to the boil and cook for 3–4 minutes. Drain and leave to cool.

Quarter or halve the cherry tomatoes and mix them into the cooled vegetables. Spread the prepared vegetables over the rice and top with the prawns. Season to taste with salt and pepper.

Cover the prawns with the mozzarella and sprinkle over the remaining Parmesan cheese. Bake in the preheated oven for 20–25 minutes until piping hot and golden brown in places. Serve immediately.

*Try this:* FOR STARTERS: 24  FOR PUDDING: 366

# Fish Crumble

**SERVES 6**

450 g/1 lb whiting or
  halibut fillets
300 ml/½ pint milk
salt and freshly ground black
  pepper
1 tbsp sunflower oil
75 g/3 oz butter or
  margarine
1 medium onion, peeled and
  finely chopped

2 leeks, trimmed and sliced
1 medium carrot, peeled and
  cut into small dice
2 medium potatoes, peeled
  and cut into small pieces
175 g/6 oz plain flour
300 ml/½ pint fish or
  vegetable stock
2 tbsp whipping cream
1 tsp freshly chopped dill

runner beans, to serve

For the crumble topping:
75 g/3 oz butter or
  margarine
175 g/6 oz plain flour
75 g/3 oz Parmesan
  cheese, grated
¾ tsp cayenne pepper

Preheat the oven to 200°C/400°F/Gas Mark 6, 15 minutes before cooking. Oil a 1.4 litre/ 2½ pint pie dish. Place the fish in a saucepan with the milk, salt and pepper. Bring to the boil, cover and simmer for 8–10 minutes until the fish is cooked. Remove with a slotted spoon, reserving the cooking liquid. Flake the fish into the prepared dish.

Heat the oil and 1 tablespoon of the butter or margarine in a small frying pan and gently fry the onion, leeks, carrot and potatoes for 1–2 minutes. Cover tightly and cook over a gentle heat for a further 10 minutes until softened. Spoon the vegetables over the fish.

Melt the remaining butter or margarine in a saucepan, add the flour and cook for 1 minute, stirring. Whisk in the reserved cooking liquid and the stock. Cook until thickened, then stir in the cream. Remove from the heat and stir in the dill. Pour over the fish.

To make the crumble, rub the butter or margarine into the flour until it resembles bread-crumbs, then stir in the cheese and cayenne pepper. Sprinkle over the dish, and bake in the preheated oven for 20 minutes until piping hot. Serve with runner beans.

*Try this:* FOR STARTERS: 56  FOR PUDDING: 352

# Potato Boulangere
# with Sea Bass

**SERVES 2**

450 g/1 lb potatoes, peeled
  and thinly sliced
1 large onion, peeled
  and thinly sliced
salt and freshly ground

black pepper
300 ml/½ pint fish or
  vegetable stock
75 g/3 oz butter or
  margarine

350 g/12 oz sea bass fillets
sprigs of fresh flat-leaf
  parsley, to garnish

Preheat the oven to 200°C/400°F/Gas Mark 6. Lightly grease a shallow 1.4 litre/2½ pint baking dish with oil or butter. Layer the potato slices and onions alternately in the prepared dish, seasoning each layer with salt and pepper.

Pour the stock over the top, then cut 50 g/2 oz of the butter or margarine into small pieces and dot over the top layer. Bake in the preheated oven for 50–60 minutes. Do not cover the dish at this stage.

Lightly rinse the sea bass fillets and pat dry on absorbent kitchen paper. Cook in a griddle, or heat the remaining butter or margarine in a frying pan and shallow fry the fish fillets for 3–4 minutes per side, flesh side first. Remove from the pan with a slotted spatula and drain on absorbent kitchen paper.

Remove the partly cooked potato and onion mixture from the oven and place the fish on the top. Cover with tinfoil and return to the oven for 10 minutes until heated through. Garnish with sprigs of parsley and serve immediately.

*Try this:* FOR STARTERS: 18   FOR PUDDING: 368

# Pork Goulash & Rice

**SERVES 4**

700 g/1½ lb boneless pork
  rib chops
1 tbsp olive oil
2 onions, peeled and
  roughly chopped
1 red pepper, deseeded and
  sliced thinly

1 garlic clove, peeled
  and crushed
1 tbsp plain flour
1 rounded tbsp paprika
400 g can chopped tomatoes
salt and freshly ground
  black pepper

250 g/9 oz long-grain
  white rice
450 ml/¾ pint chicken stock
sprigs of fresh flat-leaf
  parsley, to garnish
150 ml/¼ pint soured cream,
  to serve

Preheat the oven to 140°C/275°F/Gas Mark 1. Cut the pork into large cubes, about
4 cm/1½ inches square. Heat the oil in a large flameproof casserole and brown the pork
in batches over a high heat, transferring the cubes to a plate as they brown.

Over a medium heat, add the onions and pepper and cook for about 5 minutes, stirring regularly,
until they begin to brown. Add the garlic and return the meat to the casserole along with any
juices on the plate. Sprinkle in the flour and paprika and stir well to soak up the oil and juices.

Add the tomatoes and season to taste with salt and pepper. Bring slowly to the boil, cover with
a tight-fitting lid and cook in the preheated oven for 1½ hours.

Meanwhile, rinse the rice in several changes of water until the water remains relatively clear.
Drain well and put into a saucepan with the chicken stock or water and a little salt. Cover
tightly and bring to the boil. Turn the heat down as low as possible and cook for 10 minutes
without removing the lid. After 10 minutes, remove from the heat and leave for a further 10
minutes, without removing the lid. Fluff with a fork.

When the meat is tender, stir in the soured cream lightly to create a marbled effect, or serve
separately. Garnish with parsley and serve immediately with the rice.

*Try this:* FOR STARTERS: 32   FOR PUDDING: 356

# Roast Cured Pork Loin with Baked Sliced Potatoes

**SERVES 4**

2 tbsp wholegrain mustard
2 tbsp clear honey
1 tsp coarsely crushed
  black pepper
900 g/2 lb piece smoked
  cured pork loin

900 g/2 lb potatoes, peeled
  and thinly sliced
75 g/3 oz butter, diced
1 large onion, peeled and
  finely chopped
25 g/1 oz plain flour

salt and freshly ground
  black pepper
600 ml/1 pint milk
fresh green salad,
  to serve

Preheat the oven to 190°C/375°F/Gas Mark 5. Mix together the mustard, honey and black pepper. Spread evenly over the pork loin. Place in the centre of a large square of tinfoil and wrap loosely. Cook in the preheated oven for 15 minutes per 450 g/1 lb, plus an extra 15 minutes (45 minutes), unwrapping the joint for the last 30 minutes cooking time.

Meanwhile, layer one-third of the potatoes, one-third of the butter, half the onions and half the flour in a large gratin dish. Add half the remaining potatoes and butter and the remaining onions and flour. Finally, cover with the remaining potatoes. Season well with salt and pepper between layers. Pour in the milk and dot with the remaining butter. Cover the dish loosely with tinfoil and put in the oven below the pork. Cook for 1½ hours.

Remove the tinfoil from the potatoes and cook for a further 20 minutes until tender and golden. Remove the pork loin from the oven and leave to rest for 10 minutes before carving thinly. Serve with the potatoes and a fresh green salad.

# Shepherd's Pie

**SERVES 4**

2 tbsp vegetable or olive oil
1 onion, peeled and
　finely chopped
1 carrot, peeled and finely
　chopped
1 celery stalk, trimmed and
　finely chopped
1 tbsp sprigs of fresh thyme
450 g/1 lb leftover roast

lamb, finely chopped
150 ml/¼ pint red wine
150 ml/¼ pint lamb or
　vegetable stock or
　leftover gravy
2 tbsp tomato purée
salt and freshly ground
　black pepper
700 g/1½ lb potatoes, peeled

and cut into chunks
25 g/1 oz butter
6 tbsp milk
1 tbsp freshly
　chopped parsley
fresh herbs, to garnish

Preheat the oven to 200°C/400°F/Gas Mark 6, about 15 minutes before cooking. Heat the oil in a large saucepan and add the onion, carrot and celery. Cook over a medium heat for 8–10 minutes until softened and starting to brown.

Add the thyme and cook briefly, then add the cooked lamb, wine, stock and tomato purée. Season to taste with salt and pepper and simmer gently for 25–30 minutes until reduced and thickened. Remove from the heat to cool slightly and season again.

Meanwhile, boil the potatoes in plenty of salted water for 12–15 minutes until tender. Drain and return to the saucepan over a low heat to dry out. Remove from the heat and add the butter, milk and parsley. Mash until creamy, adding a little more milk, if necessary. Adjust the seasoning.

Transfer the lamb mixture to a shallow ovenproof dish. Spoon the mash over the filling and spread evenly to cover completely. Fork the surface, place on a baking sheet, then cook in the preheated oven for 25–30 minutes until the potato topping is browned and the filling is piping hot. Garnish and serve.

# Leg of Lamb with Minted Rice

**SERVES 4**

1 tbsp olive oil
1 medium onion, peeled and
    finely chopped
1 garlic clove, peeled
    and crushed
1 celery stalk, trimmed
    and chopped
1 large mild red chilli,
    deseeded and chopped
75 g/3 oz long-grain rice
150 ml/¼ pint lamb or
    chicken stock
2 tbsp freshly chopped mint
salt and freshly ground
    black pepper
1.4 kg/3 lb boned leg of lamb
freshly cooked vegetables,
    to serve

Preheat the oven to 190°C/375°F/Gas Mark 5, 10 minutes before roasting. Heat
the oil in a frying pan and gently cook the onion for 5 minutes. Stir in the garlic, celery
and chilli and continue to cook for 3–4 minutes.

Place the rice and the stock in a large saucepan and cook, covered, for 10–12 minutes or until the
rice is tender and all the liquid is absorbed. Stir in the onion and celery mixture, then leave to cool.
Once the rice mixture is cold, stir in the chopped mint and season to taste with salt and pepper.

Place the boned lamb skin-side down and spoon the rice mixture along the centre of the meat.
Roll up the meat to enclose the stuffing and tie securely with string. Place in a roasting tin and
roast in the preheated oven for 1 hour 20 minutes, or until cooked to personal preference.
Remove from the oven and leave to rest in a warm place for 20 minutes, before carving. Serve
with a selection of cooked vegetables.

*Try this:* FOR STARTERS: 22   FOR PUDDING: 366

# Lamb & Potato Moussaka

**SERVES 4**

700 g/1½ lb cooked
  roast lamb
700 g/1½ lb potatoes, peeled
125 g/4 oz butter
1 large onion, peeled
  and chopped
2–4 garlic cloves, peeled

and crushed
3 tbsp tomato purée
1 tbsp freshly
  chopped parsley
salt and freshly ground
  black pepper
3–4 tbsp olive oil

2 medium aubergines,
  trimmed and sliced
4 medium tomatoes, sliced
2 medium eggs
300 ml/½ pint Greek yogurt
2–3 tbsp Parmesan
  cheese, grated

Preheat the oven to 200°C/400°F/Gas Mark 6, about 15 minutes before required. Trim the lamb, discarding any fat then cut into fine dice and reserve. Thinly slice the potatoes and rinse thoroughly in cold water, then pat dry with a clean tea towel.

Melt 50 g/2 oz of the butter in a frying pan and fry the potatoes, in batches, until crisp and golden. Using a slotted spoon, remove from the pan and reserve. Use a third of the potatoes to line the base of an ovenproof dish.

Add the onion and garlic to the butter remaining in the pan and cook for 5 minutes. Add the lamb and fry for 1 minute. Blend the tomato purée with 3 tablespoons of water and stir into the pan with the parsley and salt and pepper. Spoon over the layer of potatoes, then top with the remaining potato slices.

Heat the oil and the remaining butter in the pan and brown the aubergine slices for 5–6 minutes. Arrange the tomatoes on top of the potatoes, then the aubergines on top of the tomatoes. Beat the eggs with the yogurt and Parmesan cheese and pour over the aubergine and tomatoes. Bake in the preheated oven for 25 minutes, or until golden and piping hot. Serve.

*Try this:* FOR STARTERS: 30   FOR PUDDING: 362

# Lamb Pilaf

**SERVES 4**

2 tbsp vegetable oil
25 g/1 oz flaked or
   slivered almonds
1 medium onion, peeled and
   finely chopped
1 medium carrot, peeled and
   finely chopped
1 celery stalk, trimmed and
   finely chopped
350 g/12 oz lean lamb, cut

into chunks
¼ tsp ground cinnamon
¼ tsp chilli flakes
2 large tomatoes, skinned,
   deseeded and chopped
grated rind of 1 orange
350 g/12 oz easy-cook brown
   basmati rice
600 ml/1 pint vegetable or
   lamb stock

2 tbsp freshly
   snipped chives
3 tbsp freshly
   chopped coriander
salt and freshly ground
   black pepper

To garnish:
lemon slices
sprigs of fresh coriander

Preheat the oven to 140°C/275°F/Gas Mark 1. Heat the oil in a flameproof casserole with a tight-fitting lid and add the almonds. Cook for about 1 minute until just starting to brown, stirring often. Add the onion, carrot and celery and cook gently for a further 8–10 minutes until soft and lightly browned.

Increase the heat and add the lamb. Cook for a further 5 minutes until the lamb has changed colour. Add the ground cinnamon and chilli flakes and stir briefly before adding the tomatoes and orange rind.

Stir and add the rice, then the stock. Bring slowly to the boil and cover tightly. Transfer to the preheated oven and cook for 30–35 minutes until the rice is tender and the stock is absorbed.

Remove from the oven and leave to stand for 5 minutes before stirring in the chives and coriander. Season to taste with salt and pepper. Garnish with the lemon slices and sprigs of fresh coriander and serve immediately.

*Try this:* FOR STARTERS: 36   FOR PUDDING: 378

# Roast Leg of Lamb & Boulangere Potatoes

**SERVES 6**

1.1 kg/2½ lb potatoes, peeled
1 large onion, peeled and
    finely sliced
salt and freshly ground
    black pepper
2 tbsp olive oil

50 g/2 oz butter
200 ml/7 fl oz lamb stock
100 ml/3½ fl oz milk
2 kg/4½ lb leg of lamb
2–3 sprigs of fresh rosemary
6 large garlic cloves, peeled

    and finely sliced
6 anchovy fillets, drained
extra sprigs of fresh
    rosemary, to garnish

Preheat the oven to 230°C/450°F/Gas Mark 8. Finely slice the potatoes – a mandolin is the best tool for this. Layer the potatoes with the onion in a large roasting tin, seasoning each layer with salt and pepper. Drizzle about 1 tablespoon of the olive oil over the potatoes and add the butter in small pieces. Pour in the lamb stock and milk. Set aside.

Make small incisions all over the lamb with the point of a small, sharp knife. Into each incision insert a small piece of rosemary, a sliver of garlic and a piece of anchovy fillet.

Drizzle the leg of lamb and its flavourings with the rest of the olive oil and season well. Place the meat directly onto a shelf in the preheated oven. Position the roasting tin of potatoes directly underneath to catch the juices during cooking. Roast for 15 minutes per 500 g/1 lb 2 oz (about 1 hour for a joint this size), reducing the oven temperature after 20 minutes to 200°C/400°F/Gas Mark 6.

When the lamb is cooked, remove from the oven and allow to rest for 10 minutes before carving. Meanwhile, increase the oven heat and cook the potatoes for a further 10–15 minutes to crisp up. Garnish with fresh rosemary sprigs and serve immediately with the lamb.

*Try this:* FOR STARTERS: 34   FOR PUDDING: 358

# Chilli Con Carne with Crispy–skinned Potatoes

**SERVES 4**

2 tbsp vegetable oil, plus extra for brushing
1 large onion, peeled and finely chopped
1 garlic clove, peeled and finely chopped
1 red chilli, deseeded and finely chopped

450 g/1 lb chuck steak, finely chopped, or lean beef mince
1 tbsp chilli powder
400 g can chopped tomatoes
2 tbsp tomato purée
400 g can red kidney beans, drained and rinsed

4 large baking potatoes
coarse salt and freshly ground black pepper

To serve:
ready-made guacamole
soured cream

Preheat the oven to 150°C/300°F/Gas Mark 2. Heat the oil in a large flameproof casserole dish and add the onion. Cook gently for 10 minutes until soft and lightly browned. Add the garlic and chilli and cook briefly. Increase the heat. Add the chuck steak or lean mince and cook for a further 10 minutes, stirring occasionally, until browned.

Add the chilli powder and stir well. Cook for about 2 minutes, then add the chopped tomatoes and tomato purée. Bring slowly to the boil. Cover and cook in the preheated oven for 1½ hours. Remove from the oven and stir in the kidney beans. Return to the oven for a further 15 minutes.

Meanwhile, brush a little vegetable oil all over the potatoes and rub on some coarse salt. Put the potatoes in the oven alongside the chilli.

Remove the chilli and potatoes from the oven. Cut a cross in each potato, then squeeze to open slightly and season to taste with salt and pepper. Serve with the chilli, guacamole and soured cream.

*Try this:* FOR STARTERS: 68   FOR PUDDING: 380

# Chinese Beef with Angel Hair Pasta

**SERVES 4**

1 tbsp pink peppercorns
1 tbsp chilli powder
1 tbsp Szechuan pepper
3 tbsp light soy sauce
3 tbsp dry sherry
450 g/1 lb sirloin steak,
  cut into strips

350 g/12 oz angel hair pasta
1 tbsp sesame oil
1 tbsp sunflower oil
1 bunch spring onions,
  trimmed and finely
  shredded, plus extra
  to garnish

1 red pepper, deseeded and
  thinly sliced
1 green pepper, deseeded
  and thinly sliced
1 tbsp toasted sesame
  seeds, to garnish

Crush the peppercorns, using a pestle and mortar. Transfer to a shallow bowl and combine with the chilli powder, Szechuan pepper, light soy sauce and sherry. Add the beef strips and stir until lightly coated. Cover and place in the refrigerator to marinate for 3 hours; stir occasionally during this time.

When ready to cook, bring a large pan of lightly salted water to a rolling boil. Add the pasta and cook according to the packet instructions, or until 'al dente'. Drain thoroughly and return to the pan. Add the sesame oil and toss lightly. Keep the pasta warm.

Heat a wok or large frying pan, add the sunflower oil and heat until very hot. Add the shredded spring onions with the sliced red and green peppers and stir-fry for 2 minutes.

Drain the beef, reserving the marinade, then add the beef to the wok or pan and stir-fry for 3 minutes. Pour the marinade and stir-fry for 1–2 minutes, until the steak is tender.

Pile the pasta on to four warmed plates. Top with the stir-fried beef and peppers and garnish with toasted sesame seeds and shredded spring onions. Serve immediately.

*Try this:* FOR STARTERS: 24   FOR PUDDING: 376

# Grilled Steaks with Saffron Potatoes & Roast Tomatoes

**SERVES 4**

700 g/1½ lb new
potatoes, halved
few strands of saffron
300 ml/½ pint vegetable or
beef stock
1 small onion, peeled and
finely chopped
75 g/3 oz butter
salt and freshly ground
black pepper
2 tsp balsamic vinegar
2 tbsp olive oil
1 tsp caster sugar
8 plum tomatoes, halved
4 boneless sirloin steaks,
each weighing 225 g/8 oz
2 tbsp freshly
chopped parsley

Cook the potatoes in boiling salted water for 8 minutes and drain well. Return the potatoes to the saucepan along with the saffron, stock, onion and 25 g/1 oz of the butter. Season to taste with salt and pepper and simmer, uncovered for 10 minutes until the potatoes are tender.

Meanwhile, preheat the grill to medium. Mix together the vinegar, olive oil, sugar and seasoning. Arrange the tomatoes cut-side up in a foil-lined grill pan and drizzle over the dressing. Grill for 12–15 minutes, basting occasionally, until tender.

Melt the remaining butter in a frying pan. Add the steaks and cook for 4–8 minutes to taste and depending on thickness.

Arrange the potatoes and tomatoes in the centre of four serving plates. Top with the steaks along with any pan juices. Sprinkle over the parsley and serve immediately.

*Try this:* FOR STARTERS: 42   FOR PUDDING: 378

# Beef Teriyaki with Green & Black Rice

**SERVES 4**

3 tbsp sake (Japanese
　rice wine)
3 tbsp dry sherry
3 tbsp dark soy sauce
1½ tbsp soft brown sugar
4 sirloin steaks, each

weighing 175 g/6 oz,
　trimmed
350 g/12 oz long-grain and
　wild rice
2.5 cm/1 inch piece fresh
　root ginger

225 g/8 oz mangetout
salt
6 spring onions, trimmed
　and cut into fine strips

In a small saucepan, gently heat the sake, dry sherry, dark soy sauce and sugar until the sugar has dissolved. Increase the heat and bring to the boil. Remove from the heat and leave until cold. Lightly wipe the steaks, place in a shallow dish and pour the sake mixture over. Cover loosely and leave to marinate in the refrigerator for at least 1 hour, spooning the marinade over the steaks occasionally.

Cook the rice with the piece of root ginger, according to the packet instructions. Drain well, then remove and discard the piece of ginger.

Slice the mangetout thinly lengthways into fine shreds. Plunge into a saucepan of boiling salted water, return the water to the boil and drain immediately. Stir the drained mangetout and spring onions into the hot rice.

Meanwhile, heat a griddle pan until almost smoking. Remove the steaks from the marinade and cook on the hot grill pan for 3–4 minutes each side, depending on the thickness.

Place the remaining marinade in a saucepan and bring to the boil. Simmer rapidly for 2 minutes and remove from the heat. When the steaks are cooked to personal preference, leave to rest for 2–3 minutes, then slice thinly and serve with the rice and the hot marinade.

*Try this:* FOR STARTERS: 32   FOR PUDDING: 374

# Lemon Chicken Rice

**SERVES 4**

2 tbsp sunflower oil
4 chicken leg portions
1 medium onion, peeled
   and chopped
1–2 garlic cloves, peeled
   and crushed
1 tbsp curry powder

25 g/1 oz butter
225 g/8 oz long-grain
   white rice
1 lemon, preferably
   unwaxed, sliced
600 ml/1 pint chicken stock
salt and freshly ground

black pepper
2 tbsp flaked, toasted
   almonds
sprigs of fresh coriander,
   to garnish

Preheat the oven to 180°C/350°F/Gas Mark 4, about 10 minutes before required. Heat the oil in a large frying pan, add the chicken legs and cook, turning, until sealed and golden all over. Using a slotted spoon, remove from the pan and reserve.

Add the onion and garlic to the oil remaining in the frying pan and cook for 5–7 minutes, or until just beginning to brown. Sprinkle in the curry powder and cook, stirring, for a further 1 minute. Return the chicken to the pan and stir well, then remove from the heat.

Melt the butter in a large heavy-based saucepan. Add the rice and cook, stirring, to ensure that all the grains are coated in the melted butter, then remove from the heat.

Stir the lemon slices into the chicken mixture, then spoon the mixture onto the rice and pour over the stock. Season to taste with salt and pepper.

Cover with a tight-fitting lid and cook in the preheated oven for 45 minutes, or until the rice is tender and the chicken is cooked thoroughly. Serve sprinkled with the toasted flaked almonds and sprigs of coriander.

*Try this:* FOR STARTERS: 46   FOR PUDDING: 370

# Herbed Hasselback Potatoes
## with Roast Chicken

| | | |
|---|---|---|
| 8 medium, evenly-sized potatoes, peeled | black pepper | leeks, trimmed |
| 3 large sprigs of fresh rosemary | 350 g/12 oz baby parsnips, peeled | 75 g/3 oz butter |
| 1 tbsp oil | 350 g/12 oz baby carrots, peeled | finely grated rind of 1 lemon, preferably unwaxed |
| salt and freshly ground | 350 g/12 oz baby | 1.6 kg/3½ lb chicken |

Preheat the oven to 200°C/400°F/Gas Mark 6, about 15 minutes before cooking. Place a chopstick on either side of a potato and, with a sharp knife, cut down through the potato until you reach the chopsticks; take care not to cut right through the potato. Repeat these cuts every 5 mm/¼ inch along the length of the potato. Carefully ease 2–4 of the slices apart and slip in a few rosemary sprigs. Repeat with remaining potatoes. Brush with the oil and season well with salt and pepper.

Place the seasoned potatoes in a large roasting tin. Add the parsnips, carrots and leeks to the potatoes in the tin, cover with a wire rack or trivet.

Beat the butter and lemon rind together and season to taste. Smear the chicken with the lemon butter and place on the rack over the vegetables.

Roast in the preheated oven for 1 hour 40 minutes, basting the chicken and vegetables occasionally, until cooked thoroughly. The juices should run clear when the thigh is pierced with a skewer. Place the cooked chicken on a warmed serving platter, arrange the roast vegetables around it and serve immediately.

*Try this:* FOR STARTERS: 70   FOR PUDDING: 360

# Spiced Indian Roast Potatoes with Chicken

**SERVES 4**

700 g/1½ lb waxy potatoes, peeled and cut into large chunks
salt and freshly ground black pepper
4 tbsp sunflower oil
8 chicken drumsticks
1 large Spanish onion, peeled and roughly chopped
3 shallots, peeled and roughly chopped
2 large garlic cloves, peeled and crushed
1 red chilli
2 tsp fresh root ginger, peeled and finely grated
2 tsp ground cumin
2 tsp ground coriander
pinch of cayenne pepper
4 cardamom pods, crushed
sprigs of fresh coriander, to garnish

Preheat the oven to 190°C/375°F/Gas Mark 5, about 10 minutes before cooking. Parboil the potatoes for 5 minutes in lightly salted boiling water, then drain thoroughly and reserve. Heat the oil in a large frying pan, add the chicken drumsticks and cook until sealed on all sides. Remove and reserve.

Add the onions and shallots to the pan and fry for 4–5 minutes, or until softened. Stir in the garlic, chilli and ginger and cook for 1 minute, stirring constantly. Stir in the ground cumin, coriander, cayenne pepper and crushed cardamom pods and continue to cook, stirring, for a further minute.

Add the potatoes to the pan, then add the chicken. Season to taste with salt and pepper. Stir gently until the potatoes and chicken pieces are coated in the onion and spice mixture.

Spoon into a large roasting tin and roast in the preheated oven for 35 minutes, or until the chicken and potatoes are cooked thoroughly. Garnish with fresh coriander and serve immediately.

# Pan-cooked Chicken with Thai Spices

**SERVES 4**

4 kaffir lime leaves
5 cm/2 inch piece of
    root ginger, peeled
    and chopped
300 ml/½ pint chicken
    stock, boiling
4 x 175 g/6 oz
    chicken breasts

2 tsp groundnut oil
5 tbsp coconut milk
1 tbsp fish sauce
2 red chillies, deseeded and
    finely chopped
225 g/8 oz Thai jasmine rice
1 tbsp lime juice
3 tbsp freshly

chopped coriander
salt and freshly ground
    black pepper

To garnish:
wedges of lime
freshly chopped coriander

Lightly bruise the kaffir lime leaves and put in a bowl with the chopped ginger. Pour over the chicken stock, cover and leave to infuse for 30 minutes.

Meanwhile, cut each chicken breast into two pieces. Heat the oil in a large, non-stick frying pan or flameproof casserole and brown the chicken pieces for 2–3 minutes on each side.

Strain the infused chicken stock into the pan. Half cover the pan with a lid and gently simmer for 10 minutes.

Stir in the coconut milk, fish sauce and chopped chillies. Simmer, uncovered for 5–6 minutes, or until the chicken is tender and cooked through and the sauce has reduced slightly.

Meanwhile, cook the rice in boiling salted water according to the packet instructions. Drain the rice thoroughly.

Stir the lime juice and chopped coriander into the sauce. Season to taste with salt and pepper. Serve the chicken and sauce on a bed of rice. Garnish with wedges of lime and freshly chopped coriander and serve immediately.

# Aromatic Chicken Curry

**SERVES 4**

125 g/4 oz red lentils
2 tsp ground coriander
½ tsp cumin seeds
2 tsp mild curry paste
1 bay leaf
small strip of lemon rind
600 ml/1 pint chicken or

vegetable stock
8 chicken thighs, skinned
175 g/6 oz spinach leaves,
  rinsed and shredded
1 tbsp freshly
  chopped coriander
2 tsp lemon juice

salt and freshly ground
  black pepper

To serve:
freshly cooked rice
low fat natural yogurt

Put the lentils in a sieve and rinse thoroughly under cold running water.

Dry-fry the ground coriander and cumin seeds in a large saucepan over a low heat for about 30 seconds. Stir in the curry paste.

Add the lentils to the saucepan with the bay leaf and lemon rind, then pour in the stock.

Stir, then slowly bring to the boil. Turn down the heat, half-cover the pan with a lid and simmer gently for 5 minutes, stirring occasionally.

Secure the chicken thighs with cocktail sticks to keep their shape. Place in the pan and half-cover. Simmer for 15 minutes.

Stir in the shredded spinach and cook for a further 25 minutes or until the chicken is very tender and the sauce is thick.

Remove the bay leaf and lemon rind. Stir in the coriander and lemon juice, then season to taste with salt and pepper. Serve immediately with the rice and a little natural yogurt.

*Try this:* FOR STARTERS: 50  FOR PUDDING: 356

# Chicken Cacciatore

**SERVES 4**

4 chicken leg portions
1 tbsp olive oil
1 red onion, peeled and cut
   into very thin wedges
1 garlic clove, peeled
   and crushed

sprig of fresh thyme
sprig of fresh rosemary
150 ml/¼ pint dry white wine
200 ml/7 fl oz chicken stock
400 g can chopped tomatoes
40 g/1½ oz black

olives, pitted
15 g/½ oz capers, drained
salt and freshly ground
   black pepper
freshly cooked fettuccine,
   linguine or pasta shells

Skin the chicken portions and cut each one into two pieces to make four thighs and four drumsticks.

Heat 2 teaspoons of the oil in a flameproof casserole and cook the chicken for 2–3 minutes on each side until lightly browned. Remove the chicken from the pan and reserve.

Add the remaining 1 teaspoon of oil to the juices in the pan. Add the red onion and gently cook for 5 minutes, stirring occasionally.

Add the garlic and cook for a further 5 minutes until soft and beginning to brown. Return the chicken to the pan.

Add the herbs, then pour in the wine and let it bubble for 1–2 minutes. Add the stock and tomatoes, cover and gently simmer for 15 minutes.

Stir in the olives and capers. Cook uncovered for a further 5 minutes or until the chicken is cooked and the sauce thickened. Remove the herbs and season to taste with salt and pepper.

Place the chicken on a bed of pasta, allowing one thigh and one drumstick per person. Spoon over the sauce and serve.

*Try this:* FOR STARTERS: 30  FOR PUDDING: 362

# Persian Chicken Pilaf

**SERVES 4-6**

2–3 tbsp vegetable oil
700 g/1½ lb boneless
  skinless chicken pieces
  (breast and thighs), cut
  into 2.5 cm/
  1 inch pieces
2 medium onions, peeled
  and coarsely chopped
1 tsp ground cumin

200 g/7 oz long-grain
  white rice
1 tbsp tomato purée
1 tsp saffron strands
salt and freshly ground
  black pepper
100 ml/3½ fl oz
  pomegranate juice
900 ml/1½ pints

chicken stock
125 g/4 oz ready-to-eat dried
  apricots or prunes, halved
2 tbsp raisins
2 tbsp freshly chopped mint
  or parsley
pomegranate seeds, to
  garnish (optional)

Heat the oil in a large, heavy-based saucepan over a medium-high heat. Cook the chicken pieces, in batches, until lightly browned. Return all the browned chicken to the saucepan.

Add the onions to the saucepan, reduce the heat to medium and cook for 3–5 minutes, stirring frequently, until the onions begin to soften. Add the cumin and rice and stir to coat the rice. Cook for about 2 minutes until the rice is golden and translucent. Stir in the tomato purée and the saffron strands, then season to taste with salt and pepper.

Add the pomegranate juice and stock and bring to the boil, stirring once or twice. Add the apricots or prunes and raisins and stir gently. Reduce the heat to low and cook for 30 minutes until the chicken and rice are tender and the liquid is absorbed.

Turn into a shallow serving dish and sprinkle with the chopped mint or parsley. Serve immediately, garnished with pomegranate seeds, if using.

*Try this:* FOR STARTERS: 36  FOR PUDDING: 380

# Chicken & Seafood Risotto

**SERVES 4**

125 ml/4 fl oz olive oil
1.4 kg/3 lb chicken, cut into
    8 pieces
350 g/12 oz spicy chorizo
    sausage, cut into 1 cm/½
    inch pieces
125 g/4 oz cured ham, diced
1 onion, peeled and
    chopped
2 red or yellow peppers,
    deseeded and cut into
    2.5 cm/1 inch pieces

4 garlic cloves, peeled and
    finely chopped
750 g/1 lb 10 oz short-
    grain Spanish rice or
    Arborio rice
2 bay leaves
1 tsp dried thyme
1 tsp saffron strands,
    lightly crushed
200 ml/7 fl oz dry white wine
1.6 litres/2¾ pints
    chicken stock

salt and freshly ground
    black pepper
125 g/4 oz fresh shelled peas
450 g/1 lb uncooked prawns
36 clams and/or mussels,
    well scrubbed
2 tbsp freshly
    chopped parsley

To garnish:
lemon wedges
fresh parsley sprigs

Heat half the oil in a 45.5 cm/18 inch paella pan or deep wide frying pan. Add the chicken pieces and fry for 15 minutes, turning constantly, until golden. Remove from the pan and reserve. Add the chorizo and ham to the pan and cook for 6 minutes until crisp, stirring occasionally. Remove and add to the chicken. Add the onion to the pan and cook for 3 minutes, or until beginning to soften. Add the peppers and garlic and cook for 2 minutes; add to the reserved chicken, chorizo and ham.

Add the remaining oil to the pan and stir in the rice until well coated. Stir in the bay leaves, thyme and saffron, then pour in the wine and bubble until evaporated, stirring and scraping up any bits on the bottom of the pan. Stir in the stock and bring to the boil, stirring occasionally.

Return the chicken, chorizo, ham and vegetables to the pan, burying them gently in the rice. Season to taste with salt and pepper. Reduce the heat and simmer for 10 minutes, stirring occasionally. Add the peas and seafood, pushing them gently into the rice. Cover, cook over a low heat for 5 minutes, or until the rice and prawns are tender and the clams and mussels open (discard any that do not open). Stand for 5 minutes. Sprinkle with the parsley, garnish and serve.

*Try this:* FOR STARTERS: 22  FOR PUDDING: 372

# Chicken Pie with Sweet Potato Topping

**SERVES 4**

700 g/1½ lb sweet potatoes, peeled and cut into chunks
salt and freshly ground black pepper
250 g/9 oz potatoes, peeled and cut into chunks
150 ml/¼ pint milk
25 g/1 oz butter

2 tsp brown sugar
grated rind of 1 orange
4 skinless chicken breast fillets, diced
1 medium onion, peeled and coarsely chopped
125 g/4 oz baby mushrooms, stems trimmed
2 leeks, trimmed and

thickly sliced
150 ml/¼ pint dry white wine
1 chicken stock cube
1 tbsp freshly chopped parsley
50 ml/2 fl oz crème fraîche or thick double cream
green vegetables, to serve

Preheat the oven to 190°C/375°F/Gas Mark 5, 10 minutes before required. Cook the potatoes in lightly salted boiling water until tender. Drain well, then return to the saucepan and mash until smooth and creamy, gradually adding the milk, then the butter, sugar and orange rind. Season to taste with salt and pepper and reserve.

Place the chicken in a saucepan with the onion, mushrooms, leeks, wine, stock cube and season to taste. Simmer, covered, until the chicken and vegetables are tender. Using a slotted spoon, transfer the chicken and vegetables to a 1.1 litre/2 pint pie dish. Add the parsley and crème fraîche or cream to the liquid in the pan and bring to the boil. Simmer until thickened and smooth, stirring constantly. Pour over the chicken in the pie dish, mix and cool.

Spread the mashed potato over the chicken filling, and swirl the surface into decorative peaks. Bake in the preheated oven for 35 minutes, or until the top is golden and the chicken filling is heated through. Serve immediately with fresh green vegetables.

*Try this:* FOR STARTERS: 18   FOR PUDDING: 360

# Pad Thai

**SERVES 4**

225 g/8 oz flat rice noodles
2 tbsp vegetable oil
225 g/8 oz boneless chicken breast, skinned and thinly sliced
4 shallots, peeled and thinly sliced
2 garlic cloves, peeled and finely chopped
4 spring onions, trimmed and diagonally cut into

5 cm/2 inch pieces
350 g/12 oz fresh white crab meat or tiny prawns
75 g/3 oz fresh bean sprouts, rinsed and drained
2 tbsp preserved or fresh radish, chopped
2–3 tbsp roasted peanuts, chopped (optional)

For the sauce:
3 tbsp Thai fish sauce (nam pla)
2–3 tbsp rice vinegar or cider vinegar
1 tbsp chilli bean or oyster sauce
1 tbsp toasted sesame oil
1 tbsp light brown sugar
1 red chilli, deseeded and thinly sliced

To make the sauce, whisk all the sauce ingredients in a bowl and reserve. Put the rice noodles in a large bowl and pour over enough hot water to cover. Leave to stand for about 15 minutes until softened. Drain and rinse, then drain again.

Heat the oil in a wok over a high heat until hot, but not smoking. Add the chicken strips and stir-fry constantly until they begin to colour. Using a slotted spoon, transfer to a plate. Reduce the heat to medium-high.

Add the shallots, garlic and spring onions and stir-fry for 1 minute. Stir in the rice noodles, then the reserved sauce; mix well.

Add the reserved chicken strips, with the crab meat or prawns, bean sprouts and radish and stir well. Cook for about 5 minutes, stirring frequently, until heated through. If the noodles begin to stick, add a little water.

Turn into a large shallow serving dish and sprinkle with the chopped peanuts, if desired. Serve immediately.

*Try this:* FOR STARTERS: 32  FOR PUDDING: 376

# Turkey & Tomato Tagine

**SERVES 4**

**For the meatballs:**
450 g/1 lb fresh turkey mince
1 small onion, peeled and
   very finely chopped
1 garlic clove, peeled
   and crushed
1 tbsp freshly
   chopped coriander
1 tsp ground cumin
1 tbsp olive oil

salt and freshly ground
   black pepper

**For the sauce:**
1 onion, peeled and
   finely chopped
1 garlic clove, peeled
   and crushed
150 ml/¼ pint turkey stock
400 g can chopped tomatoes

½ tsp ground cumin
½ tsp ground cinnamon
pinch of cayenne pepper
freshly chopped parsley
freshly chopped herbs,
   to garnish
freshly cooked couscous or
   rice, to serve

Preheat the oven to 190°C/375°F/Gas Mark 5. Put all the ingredients for the meatballs in a bowl, except the oil and mix well. Season to taste with salt and pepper. Shape into 20 balls, about the size of walnuts. Put on a tray, cover lightly and chill in the refrigerator while making the sauce.

Put the onion and garlic in a pan with 125 ml/4 fl oz of the stock. Cook over a low heat until all the stock has evaporated. Continue cooking for 1 minute, or until the onions begin to colour. Add the remaining stock to the pan with the tomatoes, cumin, cinnamon and cayenne pepper. Simmer for 10 minutes, until slightly thickened and reduced. Stir in the parsley and season to taste.

Heat the oil in a large non-stick frying pan and cook the meatballs in two batches until lightly browned all over. Lift the meatballs out with a slotted spoon and drain on kitchen paper.

Pour the sauce into a tagine or an ovenproof casserole. Top with the meatballs, cover and cook in the preheated oven for 25–30 minutes, or until the meatballs are cooked through and the sauce is bubbling. Garnish with freshly chopped herbs and serve immediately on a bed of couscous or plain boiled rice.

*Try this:* FOR STARTERS: 42   FOR PUDDING: 380

# Turkey Escalopes with Apricot Chutney

**SERVES 4**

4 x 175–225 g/6–8 oz
   turkey steaks
1 tbsp plain flour
salt and freshly ground
   black pepper
1 tbsp olive oil
flat-leaf parsley sprigs,
   to garnish

orange wedges, to serve

For the apricot chutney:
125 g/4 oz no-need-to-soak
   dried apricots, chopped
1 red onion, peeled and
   finely chopped
1 tsp grated fresh root ginger

2 tbsp caster sugar
finely grated rind of ½
   orange
125 ml/4 fl oz fresh
   orange juice
125 ml/4 fl oz ruby port
1 whole clove

Put a turkey steak on to a sheet of non-pvc clingfilm or non-stick baking parchment. Cover with a second sheet. Using a rolling pin, gently pound the turkey until the meat is flattened to about 5 mm/ ¼ inch thick. Repeat to make 4 escalopes.

Mix the flour with the salt and pepper and use to lightly dust the turkey escalopes. Put the turkey escalopes on a board or baking tray and cover with a piece of non-pvc clingfilm or non-stick baking parchment. Chill in the refrigerator until ready to cook.

For the apricot chutney, put the apricots, onion, ginger, sugar, orange rind, orange juice, port and clove into a saucepan.

Slowly bring to the boil and simmer, uncovered for 10 minutes, stirring occasionally, until thick and syrupy. Remove the clove and stir in the chopped coriander.

Heat the oil in a pan and chargriddle the turkey escalopes, in two batches if necessary, for 3–4 minutes on each side until golden brown and tender.

Spoon the chutney on to four individual serving plates. Place a turkey escalope on top of each spoonful of chutney. Garnish with sprigs of parsley and serve immediately with orange wedges.

*Try this:* FOR STARTERS: 68    FOR PUDDING: 364

# Smoked Turkey Tagliatelle

**SERVES 4**

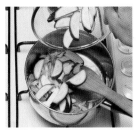

2 tsp olive oil
1 bunch spring onions,
  trimmed and
  diagonally sliced
1 garlic clove, peeled
  and crushed
1 small courgette, trimmed,

sliced and cut in half
4 tbsp dry white wine
400 g can chopped tomatoes
2 tbsp freshly shredded basil
salt and freshly ground
  black pepper
225 g/8 oz spinach and

egg tagliatelle
225 g/8 oz smoked turkey
  breast, cut into strips
small fresh basil leaves,
  to garnish

Heat the oil in a saucepan. Add the spring onions and garlic and gently cook for 2–3 minutes, until beginning to soften. Stir in the sliced courgette and cook for 1 minute.

Add the wine and let it bubble for 1–2 minutes. Stir in the chopped tomatoes, bring to the boil and simmer uncovered over a low heat for 15 minutes, or until the courgettes are tender and the sauce slightly reduced. Stir the shredded basil into the sauce and season to taste with salt and pepper.

Meanwhile, bring a large pan of salted water to the boil. Add the tagliatelle and cook for 10 minutes, until al dente or according to the packet instructions. Drain thoroughly.

Return the tagliatelle to the pan, add half the tomato sauce and toss together to coat the pasta thoroughly in the sauce. Cover with a lid and reserve.

Add the strips of turkey to the remaining sauce and heat gently for 2–3 minutes until piping hot. Divide the tagliatelle among four serving plates. Spoon over the sauce, garnish with basil leaves and serve immediately.

*Try this:* FOR STARTERS: 22   FOR PUDDING: 378

# Turkey Hash with Potato & Beetroot

**SERVES 4-6**

| | | |
|---|---|---|
| 2 tbsp vegetable oil | 450 g/1 lb cooked | 2 tbsp plain flour |
| 50 g/2 oz butter | turkey, diced | 250 g/9 oz cooked medium |
| 4 slices streaky bacon, diced | 450 g/1 lb finely chopped | beetroot, diced |
| or sliced | cooked potatoes | green salad, to serve |
| 1 medium onion, peeled and | 2–3 tbsp freshly | |
| finely chopped | chopped parsley | |

In a large, heavy-based frying pan, heat the oil and half the butter over a medium heat until sizzling. Add the bacon and cook for 4 minutes, or until crisp and golden, stirring occasionally. Using a slotted spoon, transfer to a large bowl. Add the onion to the pan and cook for 3–4 minutes, or until soft and golden, stirring frequently.

Meanwhile, add the turkey, potatoes, parsley and flour to the cooked bacon in the bowl. Stir and toss gently, then fold in the diced beetroot.

Add half the remaining butter to the frying pan and then the turkey vegetable mixture. Stir, then spread the mixture to evenly cover the bottom of the frying pan. Cook for 15 minutes, or until the underside is crisp and brown, pressing the hash firmly into a cake with a spatula. Remove from the heat.

Invert a large plate over the frying pan and, holding the plate and frying pan together with an oven glove, turn the hash out onto the plate. Heat the remaining butter in the pan, slide the hash back into the pan and cook for 4 minutes, or until crisp and brown on the other side. Invert onto the plate again and serve immediately with a green salad.

*Try this:* FOR STARTERS: 28   FOR PUDDING: 356

# Turkey & Pesto Rice Roulades

**SERVES 4**

125 g/4 oz cooked white rice, at room temperature
1 garlic clove, peeled and crushed
1–2 tbsp Parmesan cheese, grated
2 tbsp prepared pesto sauce
2 tbsp pine nuts, lightly

toasted and chopped
4 turkey steaks, each weighing about 150 g/5 oz
salt and freshly ground black pepper
4 slices Parma ham
2 tbsp olive oil
50 ml/2 fl oz white wine

25 g/1 oz unsalted butter, chilled

To serve:
freshly cooked spinach
freshly cooked pasta

Put the rice in a bowl and add the garlic, Parmesan cheese, pesto and pine nuts. Stir to combine the ingredients, then reserve.

Place the turkey steaks on a chopping board and, using a sharp knife, cut horizontally through each steak, without cutting right through. Open up the steaks and cover with baking parchment. Flatten slightly by pounding with a meat mallet or rolling pin.

Season each steak with salt and pepper. Divide the stuffing equally among the steaks, spreading evenly over one half. Fold the steaks in half to enclose the filling, then wrap each steak in a slice of Parma ham and secure with cocktail sticks.

Heat the oil in a large frying pan over medium heat. Cook the steaks for 5 minutes, or until golden on one side. Turn and cook for a further 2 minutes. Push the steaks to the side and pour in the wine. Allow the wine to bubble and evaporate. Add the butter, a little at a time, whisking constantly until the sauce is smooth. Discard the cocktail sticks, then serve the steaks drizzled with the sauce and serve with spinach and pasta.

*Try this:* FOR STARTERS: 36  FOR PUDDING: 368

# Turkey & Mixed Mushroom Lasagne

**SERVES 4**

1 tbsp olive oil
225 g/8 oz mixed
   mushrooms e.g. button,
   chestnut and portabello,
   wiped and sliced
15 g/½ oz butter
25 g/1 oz plain flour
300 ml/½ pint skimmed milk
1 bay leaf
225 g/8 oz cooked

turkey, cubed
¼ tsp freshly grated nutmeg
salt and freshly ground
   black pepper
400 g can plum tomatoes,
   drained and chopped
1 tsp dried mixed herbs
9 lasagne sheets (about
   150 g/5 oz)

For the topping:
200 ml/7 fl oz 0%-fat
   Greek yogurt
1 medium egg,
   lightly beaten
1 tbsp finely grated
   Parmesan cheese
mixed salad leaves,
   to serve

Preheat the oven to 180°C/350°F/Gas 4. Heat the oil and cook the mushrooms until tender and all the juices have evaporated. Remove and reserve.

Put the butter, flour, milk and bay leaf in the pan. Slowly bring to the boil, stirring until thickened. Simmer for 2–3 minutes. Remove the bay leaf and stir in the mushrooms, turkey, nutmeg, salt and pepper.

Mix together the tomatoes, mixed herbs and season with salt and pepper. Spoon half into the base of a 1.7 litre/3 pint ovenproof dish. Top with 3 sheets of lasagne, then with half the turkey mixture. Repeat the layers, then arrange the remaining 3 sheets of pasta on top.

Mix together the yogurt and egg. Spoon over the lasagne, spreading the mixture into the corners. Sprinkle with the Parmesan and bake in the preheated oven for 45 minutes. Serve with the mixed salad.

*Try this*: FOR STARTERS: 22   FOR PUDDING: 354

# Fried Ginger Rice with Soy Glazed Duck

**SERVES 4–6**

2 duck breasts, skinned
  and diagonally cut into
  thin slices
2–3 tbsp Japanese soy sauce
1 tbsp mirin (sweet rice
  wine) or sherry
2 tbsp brown sugar
5 cm/2 inch piece of fresh
  root ginger, peeled and
  finely chopped

4 tbsp peanut or vegetable oil
2 garlic cloves, peeled
  and crushed
300 g/11 oz long-grain
  brown rice
900 ml/1½ pints
  chicken stock
freshly ground black pepper
125 g/4 oz lean ham, diced
175 g/6 oz mangetout,

diagonally cut in half
8 spring onions, trimmed
  and diagonally
  thinly sliced
1 tbsp freshly chopped
  coriander
sweet or hot chilli sauce,
  to taste (optional)
sprigs of fresh coriander,
  to garnish

Put the duck slices in a bowl with 1 tablespoon of the soy sauce, the mirin, 1 teaspoon of the sugar and one-third of the ginger; stir. Leave to stand.

Heat 2 tablespoons of the oil in a large heavy-based saucepan. Add the garlic and half the remaining ginger and stir-fry for 1 minute. Add the rice and cook for 3 minutes, stirring constantly, until translucent. Stir in all but 125 ml/4 fl oz of the stock, with 1 teaspoon of the soy sauce, and bring to the boil. Season with pepper. Reduce the heat to very low and simmer, covered, for 25–30 minutes until the rice is tender and the liquid is absorbed. Cover and leave to stand.

Heat the remaining oil in a large frying pan or wok. Drain the duck strips and add to the frying pan. Stir-fry for 2–3 minutes until just coloured. Add 1 tablespoon of soy sauce and the remaining sugar and cook for 1 minute until glazed. Transfer to a plate and keep warm.

Stir in the ham, mangetout, spring onions, the remaining ginger and the chopped coriander. Add the remaining stock and duck marinade and cook until the liquid is almost reduced. Fork in the rice and a little chilli sauce to taste (if using); stir well. Turn into a serving dish and top with the duck. Garnish with coriander sprigs and serve immediately.

# Vegetarian

# Sicilian Baked Aubergine

**SERVES 4**

1 large aubergine, trimmed
2 celery stalks, trimmed
4 large ripe tomatoes
1 tsp sunflower oil
2 shallots, peeled and
    finely chopped

1½ tsp tomato purée
25 g/1 oz green pitted olives
25 g/1 oz black pitted olives
salt and freshly ground
    black pepper
1 tbsp white wine vinegar

2 tsp caster sugar
1 tbsp freshly chopped basil,
    to garnish
mixed salad leaves, to serve

Preheat the oven to 200°C/400°F/Gas Mark 6. Cut the aubergine into small cubes and place on an oiled baking tray.

Cover the tray with tinfoil and bake in the preheated oven for 15–20 minutes until soft. Reserve, to allow the aubergine to cool.

Place the celery and tomatoes in a large bowl and cover with boiling water. Remove the tomatoes from the bowl when their skins begin to peel away. Remove the skins then, deseed and chop the flesh into small pieces. Remove the celery from the bowl of water, finely chop and reserve.

Pour the vegetable oil into a non-stick saucepan, add the chopped shallots and fry gently for 2–3 minutes until soft. Add the celery, tomatoes, tomato purée and olives. Season to taste with salt and pepper.

Simmer gently for 3–4 minutes. Add the vinegar, sugar and cooled aubergine to the pan and heat gently for 2–3 minutes until all the ingredients are well blended. Reserve to allow the aubergine mixture to cool. When cool, garnish with the chopped basil and serve cold with salad leaves.

*Try this:* FOR STARTERS: 22   FOR PUDDING: 376

# Light Ratatouille

**SERVES 4**

1 red pepper
2 courgettes, trimmed
1 small aubergine, trimmed
1 onion, peeled

2 ripe tomatoes
50 g/2 oz button
   mushrooms, wiped
   and halved or quartered

200 ml/7 fl oz tomato juice
1 tbsp freshly chopped basil
salt and freshly ground
   black pepper

Deseed the peppers, remove the membrane with a small sharp knife and cut into small dice. Thickly slice the courgettes and cut the aubergine into small dice. Slice the onion into rings.

Place the tomatoes in boiling water until their skins begin to peel away. Remove the skins from the tomatoes, cut into quarters and remove the seeds.

Place all the vegetables in a saucepan with the tomato juice and basil. Season to taste with salt and pepper.

Bring to the boil, cover and simmer for 15 minutes or until the vegetables are tender. Remove the vegetables with a slotted spoon and arrange in a serving dish.

Bring the liquid in the pan to the boil and boil for 20 seconds until it is slightly thickened. Season the sauce to taste with salt and pepper.

Pass the sauce through a sieve to remove some of the seeds and pour over the vegetables. Serve the ratatouille hot or cold.

*Try this:* FOR STARTERS: 26   FOR PUDDING: 370

# Aduki Bean & Rice Burgers

**SERVES 4**

2½ tbsp sunflower oil
1 medium onion, peeled and
   very finely chopped
1 garlic clove, peeled
   and crushed
1 tsp curry paste
225 g/8 oz basmati rice
400 g can aduki beans,
   drained and rinsed
225 ml/8 fl oz
vegetable stock

125 g/4 oz firm tofu,
   crumbled
1 tsp garam masala
2 tbsp freshly chopped
   coriander
salt and freshly ground
   black pepper

For the carrot raita:
2 large carrots, peeled
   and grated

½ cucumber, cut into
   tiny dice
150 ml/¼ pint Greek yogurt

To serve:
wholemeal baps
tomato slices
lettuce leaves

Heat 1 tablespoon of the oil in a saucepan and gently cook the onion for 10 minutes until soft. Add the garlic and curry paste and cook for a few more seconds. Stir in the rice and beans.

Pour in the stock, bring to the boil and simmer for 12 minutes, or until all the stock has been absorbed – do not lift the lid for the first 10 minutes of cooking. Reserve.

Lightly mash the tofu. Add to the rice mixture with the garam masala, coriander, salt and pepper. Mix. Divide the mixture into eight and shape into burgers. Chill in the refrigerator for 30 minutes.

Meanwhile, make the raita. Mix together the carrots, cucumber and Greek yogurt. Spoon into a small bowl and chill in the refrigerator until ready to serve.

Heat the remaining oil in a large frying pan. Fry the burgers, in batches if necessary, for 4–5 minutes on each side, or until lightly browned. Serve in the baps with tomato slices and lettuce. Accompany with the raita.

*Try this:* FOR STARTERS: 24   FOR PUDDING: 358

# Rice Nuggets in Herby Tomato Sauce

**SERVES 4**

600 ml/1 pint
    vegetable stock
1 bay leaf
175 g/6 oz Arborio rice
50 g/2 oz Cheddar
    cheese, grated
1 medium egg yolk
1 tbsp plain flour

2 tbsp freshly
    chopped parsley
salt and freshly ground
    black pepper
grated Parmesan cheese,
    to serve
For the herby tomato sauce:
1 tbsp olive oil

1 onion, peeled and
    thinly sliced
1 garlic clove, peeled
    and crushed
1 small yellow pepper,
    deseeded and diced
400 g can chopped tomatoes
1 tbsp freshly chopped basil

Pour the stock into a large saucepan. Add the bay leaf. Bring to the boil, add the rice, stir, then cover and simmer for 15 minutes.

Uncover, reduce the heat to low and cook for a further 5 minutes until the rice is tender and all the stock is absorbed, stirring frequently towards the end of cooking time. Cool.

Stir the cheese, egg yolk, flour and parsley into the rice. Season to taste, then shape into 20 walnut-sized balls. Cover and refrigerate.

To make the sauce, heat the oil in a large frying pan and cook the onion for 5 minutes. Add the garlic and yellow pepper and cook for a further 5 minutes, until soft.

Stir in the chopped tomatoes and simmer gently for 3 minutes. Stir in the chopped basil and season to taste.

Add the rice nuggets to the sauce and simmer for a further 10 minutes, or until the rice nuggets are cooked through and the sauce has reduced a little. Spoon onto serving plates and serve hot, sprinkled with grated Parmesan cheese.

*Try this:* FOR STARTERS: 36   FOR PUDDING: 352

# Warm Leek & Tomato Salad

**SERVES 4**

450 g/1 lb trimmed
    baby leeks
225 g/8 oz ripe, but
    firm tomatoes
2 shallots, peeled and cut
    into thin wedges

For the honey and
    lime dressing:
2 tbsp clear honey
grated rind of 1 lime
4 tbsp lime juice
1 tbsp light olive oil
1 tsp Dijon mustard

salt and freshly
    ground black pepper

To garnish:
freshly chopped tarragon
freshly chopped basil

Trim the leeks so that they are all the same length. Place in a steamer over a pan of boiling water and steam for 8 minutes or until just tender.

Drain the leeks thoroughly and arrange in a shallow serving dish.

Make a cross in the top of the tomatoes, place in a bowl and cover them with boiling water until their skins start to peel away. Remove from the bowl and carefully remove the skins.

Cut the tomatoes into four and remove the seeds, then chop into small dice. Spoon over the top of the leeks together with the shallots.

In a small bowl make the dressing by whisking the honey, lime rind, lime juice, olive oil, mustard and salt and pepper. Pour 3 tablespoons of the dressing over the leeks and tomatoes and garnish with the tarragon and basil. Serve while the leeks are still warm, with the remaining dressing served separately.

*Try this:* FOR STARTERS: 28   FOR PUDDING: 356

# Spanish Baked Tomatoes

**SERVES 4**

175 g/6 oz whole-grain rice
600 ml/1 pint
   vegetable stock
2 tsp sunflower oil
2 shallots, peeled and
   finely chopped
1 garlic clove, peeled
   and crushed

1 green pepper, deseeded
   and cut into small dice
1 red chilli, deseeded and
   finely chopped
50 g/2 oz button mushrooms
   finely chopped
1 tbsp freshly
   chopped oregano

salt and freshly ground
   black pepper
4 large ripe beef tomatoes
1 large egg, beaten
1 tsp caster sugar
basil leaves, to garnish
crusty bread, to serve

Preheat the oven to 180°C/350°F/Gas Mark 4. Place the rice in a saucepan, pour over the vegetable stock and bring to the boil. Simmer for 30 minutes or until the rice is tender. Drain and turn into a mixing bowl.

Add 1 teaspoon of sunflower oil to a small, non-stick pan and gently fry the shallots, garlic, pepper, chilli and mushrooms for 2 minutes. Add to the rice with the chopped oregano. Season with plenty of salt and pepper.

Slice the top off each tomato. Cut and scoop out the flesh, removing the hard core. Pass the tomato flesh through a sieve. Add 1 tablespoon of the juice to the rice mixture. Stir in the beaten egg and mix. Sprinkle a little sugar in the base of each tomato. Pile the rice mixture into the shells.

Place the tomatoes in a baking dish and pour a little cold water around them. Replace their lids and drizzle a few drops of sunflower oil over the tops.

Bake in the preheated oven for about 25 minutes. Garnish with the basil leaves and season with black pepper and serve immediately with crusty bread.

# Stuffed Onions with Pine Nuts

**SERVES 4**

4 medium onions, peeled
2 garlic cloves, peeled
 and crushed
2 tbsp fresh
 brown breadcrumbs
2 tbsp white breadcrumbs

25 g/1 oz sultanas
25 g/1 oz pine nuts
50 g/2 oz low fat hard
 cheese such as
 Edam, grated
2 tbsp freshly

chopped parsley
1 medium egg, beaten
salt and freshly ground
 black pepper
salad leaves,
 to serve

Preheat the oven to 200°C/400°F/Gas Mark 6. Bring a pan of water to the boil, add the onions and cook gently for about 15 minutes.

Drain well. Allow the onions to cool, then slice each one in half horizontally. Scoop out most of the onion flesh but leave a reasonably firm shell.

Chop up 4 tablespoons of the onion flesh and place in a bowl with the crushed garlic, breadcrumbs, sultanas, pine nuts, grated cheese and parsley.

Mix the breadcrumb mixture together thoroughly. Bind together with as much of the beaten egg as necessary to make a firm filling. Season to taste with salt and pepper.

Pile the mixture back into the onion shells and top with the grated cheese. Place on a oiled baking tray and cook in the preheated oven for 20–30 minutes or until golden brown. Serve immediately with the salad leaves.

# Potato & Goats' Cheese Tart

**SERVES 4**

275 g/10 oz prepared shortcrust pastry, thawed if frozen
550 g/1¼ lb small waxy potatoes
salt and freshly ground black pepper

beaten egg, for brushing
2 tbsp sun-dried tomato paste
¼ tsp chilli powder, or to taste
1 large egg
150 ml/¼ pint soured cream

150 ml/¼ pint milk
2 tbsp freshly snipped chives
300 g/11 oz goats' cheese, sliced
salad and warm crusty bread, to serve

Preheat the oven to 190°C/375°F/Gas Mark 5, about 10 minutes before cooking. Roll the pastry out on a lightly floured surface and use to line a 23 cm/9 inch fluted flan tin. Chill in the refrigerator for 30 minutes.

Scrub the potatoes, place in a large saucepan of lightly salted water and bring to the boil. Simmer for 10–15 minutes, or until the potatoes are tender. Drain and reserve until cool enough to handle.

Line the pastry case with greaseproof paper and baking beans or crumpled tinfoil and bake blind in the preheated oven for 15 minutes. Remove from the oven and discard the paper and beans or tinfoil. Brush the base with a little beaten egg, then return to the oven and cook for a further 5 minutes. Remove from the oven.

Cut the potatoes into 1 cm/½ inch thick slices and reserve. Spread the sun-dried tomato paste over the base of pastry case, sprinkle with the chilli powder, then arrange the potato slices on top in a decorative pattern.

Beat together the egg, soured cream, milk and chives, then season to taste with salt and pepper. Pour over the potatoes. Arrange the goats' cheese on top of the potatoes. Bake in the preheated oven for 30 minutes until golden brown and set. Serve immediately with salad and warm bread.

*Try this:* FOR STARTERS: 42   FOR PUDDING: 362

# Thai Noodles & Vegetables with Tofu

**SERVES 4**

225 g/8 oz firm tofu
2 tbsp soy sauce
rind of 1 lime, grated
2 lemon grass stalks
1 red chilli
1 litre/1¾ pint
    vegetable stock
2 slices fresh root
    ginger, peeled

2 garlic cloves, peeled
2 sprigs of fresh coriander
175 g/6 oz dried thread
    egg noodles
125 g/4 oz shiitake or button
    mushrooms, sliced
    if large
2 carrots, peeled and
    cut into matchsticks

125 g/4 oz mangetout
125 g/4 oz pak choi or
    other Chinese leaf
1 tbsp freshly
    chopped coriander
salt and freshly ground
    black pepper
coriander sprigs, to garnish

Drain the tofu well and cut into cubes. Put into a shallow dish with the soy sauce and lime rind. Stir well to coat and leave to marinate for 30 minutes.

Meanwhile, put the lemon grass and chilli on a chopping board and bruise with the side of a large knife, ensuring the blade is pointing away from you. Put the vegetable stock in a large saucepan and add the lemon grass, chilli, ginger, garlic, and coriander. Bring to the boil, cover and simmer gently for 20 minutes.

Strain the stock into a clean pan. Return to the boil and add the noodles, tofu and its marinade and the mushrooms. Simmer gently for 4 minutes.

Add the carrots, mangetout, pak choi, coriander and simmer for a further 3–4 minutes until the vegetables are just tender. Season to taste with salt and pepper. Garnish with coriander sprigs. Serve immediately.

# Tagliatelle with Broccoli & Sesame

**SERVES 2**

225 g/8 oz broccoli,
   cut into florets
125 g/4 oz baby corn
175 g/6 oz dried tagliatelle
1½ tbsp tahini paste
1 tbsp dark soy sauce
1 tbsp dark

muscovado sugar
1 tbsp red wine vinegar
1 tbsp sunflower oil
1 garlic clove, peeled
   and finely chopped
2.5 cm/1 inch piece fresh
   root ginger, peeled

and shredded
½ tsp dried chilli flakes
salt and freshly ground
   black pepper
1 tbsp toasted sesame seeds
slices of radish, to garnish

Bring a large saucepan of salted water to the boiland add the broccoli and corn. Return the water to the boil then remove the vegetables at once using a slotted spoon, reserving the water. Plunge them into cold water and drain well. Dry on kitchen paper and reserve.

Return the water to the boil. Add the tagliatelle and cook until al dente or according to the packet instructions. Drain well. Run under cold water until cold, then drain well again.

Place the tahini, soy sauce, sugar and vinegar into a bowl. Mix well, then reserve. Heat the oil in a wok or large frying pan over a high heat and add the garlic, ginger and chilli flakes and stir-fry for about 30 seconds. Add the broccoli and baby corn and continue to stir-fry for about 3 minutes.

Add the tagliatelle to the wok along with the tahini mixture and stir together for a further 1–2 minutes until heated through. Season to taste with salt and pepper. Sprinkle with sesame seeds, garnish with the radish slices and serve immediately.

*Try this:* FOR STARTERS: 24  FOR PUDDING: 380

# Baby Roast Potato Salad

**SERVES 4**

350 g/12 oz small shallots
sea salt and freshly ground
    black pepper
900 g/2 lb small even-sized
    new potatoes

2 tbsp olive oil
2 medium courgettes
2 sprigs of fresh rosemary
175 g/6 oz cherry tomatoes
150 ml/¼ pint soured cream

2 tbsp freshly
    snipped chives
¼ tsp paprika

Preheat the oven to 200˚C/400˚F/Gas Mark 6. Trim the shallots, but leave the skins on. Put in a saucepan of lightly salted boiling water with the potatoes and cook for 5 minutes; drain. Separate the shallots and plunge them into cold water for 1 minute.

Put the oil in a baking sheet lined with tinfoil or roasting tin and heat for a few minutes. Peel the skins off the shallots – they should now come away easily. Add to the baking sheet or roasting tin with the potatoes and toss in the oil to coat. Sprinkle with a little sea salt. Roast the potatoes and shallots in the preheated oven for 10 minutes.

Meanwhile, trim the courgettes, halve lengthways and cut into 5 cm/2 inch chunks. Add to the baking sheet or roasting tin, toss to mix and cook for 5 minutes.

Pierce the tomato skins with a sharp knife. Add to the sheet or tin with the rosemary and cook for a further 5 minutes, or until all the vegetables are tender. Remove the rosemary and discard. Grind a little black pepper over the vegetables.

Spoon into a wide serving bowl. Mix together the soured cream and chives and drizzle over the vegetables just before serving.

# Pasta with Courgettes, Rosemary & Lemon

**SERVES 4**

350 g/12 oz dried pasta
   shapes, e.g. rigatoni
1½ tbsp good quality
   extra virgin olive oil
2 garlic cloves, peeled
   and finely chopped
4 medium courgettes,
   thinly sliced

1 tbsp freshly
   chopped rosemary
1 tbsp freshly
   chopped parsley
zest and juice of 2 lemons
25 g/1 oz pitted black olives,
   roughly chopped
25 g/1 oz pitted green olives,

roughly chopped
salt and freshly ground
   black pepper

To garnish:
lemon slices
sprigs of fresh rosemary

Bring a large saucepan of salted water to the boil and add the pasta. Return to the boil and cook until 'al dente' or according to the packet instructions.

Meanwhile, when the pasta is almost done, heat the oil in a large frying pan and add the garlic.

Cook over a medium heat until the garlic just begins to brown. Be careful not to overcook the garlic at this stage or it will become bitter.

Add the courgettes, rosemary, parsley and lemon zest and juice. Cook for 3–4 minutes until the courgettes are just tender.

Add the olives to the frying pan and stir well. Season to taste with salt and pepper and remove from the heat.

Drain the pasta well and add to the frying pan. Stir until thoroughly combined. Garnish with lemon and sprigs of fresh rosemary and serve immediately.

*Try this:* FOR STARTERS: 22   FOR PUDDING: 360

# Vegetarian Spaghetti Bolognese

**SERVES 4**

2 tbsp olive oil
1 onion, peeled and
   finely chopped
1 carrot, peeled and
   finely chopped
1 celery stick, trimmed and
   finely chopped

225 g/8 oz Quorn mince
150 ml/5 fl oz red wine
300 ml/½ pint
   vegetable stock
1 tsp mushroom ketchup
4 tbsp tomato purée
350 g/12 oz dried spaghetti

4 tbsp half-fat crème fraîche
salt and freshly ground
   black pepper
1 tbsp freshly
   chopped parsley

Heat the oil in a large saucepan and add the onion, carrot and celery. Cook gently for 10 minutes, adding a little water if necessary, until softened and starting to brown.

Add the Quorn mince and cook a further 2–3 minutes before adding the red wine. Increase the heat and simmer gently until nearly all the wine has evaporated.

Mix together the vegetable stock and mushroom ketchup and add about half to the Quorn mixture along with the tomato purée. Cover and simmer gently for about 45 minutes, adding the remaining stock as necessary.

Meanwhile, bring a large pan of salted water to the boil and add the spaghetti. Cook until al dente or according to the packet instructions. Drain well. Remove the sauce from the heat, add the crème fraîche and season to taste with salt and pepper. Stir in the parsley and serve immediately with the pasta.

*Try this:* FOR STARTERS: 66   FOR PUDDING: 376

# Spring Vegetable & Herb Risotto

**SERVES 2-3**

1 litre/1¾ pint
  vegetable stock
125 g/4 oz asparagus
  tips, trimmed
125 g/4 oz baby
  carrots, scrubbed
50 g/2 oz peas, fresh
  or frozen

50 g/2 oz fine French
  beans, trimmed
1 tbsp olive oil
1 onion, peeled and
  finely chopped
1 garlic clove, peeled and
  finely chopped
2 tsp freshly chopped thyme

225 g/8 oz risotto rice
150 ml/¼ pint white wine
1 tbsp each freshly chopped
  basil, chives and parsley
zest of ½ lemon
3 tbsp half-fat crème fraîche
salt and freshly ground
  black pepper

Bring the vegetable stock to the boil in a large saucepan and add the asparagus, baby carrots, peas and beans. Bring the stock back to the boil and remove the vegetables at once using a slotted spoon. Rinse under cold running water. Drain again and reserve. Keep the stock hot.

Heat the oil in a large deep frying pan and add the onion. Cook over a medium heat for 4–5 minutes until starting to brown. Add the garlic and thyme and cook for a further few seconds. Add the rice and stir well for a minute until the rice is hot and coated in oil.

Add the white wine and stir constantly until the wine is almost completely absorbed by the rice. Begin adding the stock a ladleful at a time, stirring well and waiting until the last ladleful has been absorbed before stirring in the next. Add the vegetables after using about half of the stock. Continue until all the stock is used. This will take 20–25 minutes. The rice and vegetables should both be tender.

Remove the pan from the heat. Stir in the herbs, lemon zest and crème fraîche. Season to taste with salt and pepper and serve immediately.

*Try this:* FOR STARTERS: 18   FOR PUDDING: 372

# Vegetable Biryani

## SERVES 4

2 tbsp vegetable oil, plus a little extra for brushing
2 large onions, peeled and thinly sliced lengthwise
2 garlic cloves, peeled and finely chopped
2.5 cm/1 inch piece fresh root ginger, peeled and finely grated
1 small carrot, peeled and cut into sticks

1 small parsnip, peeled and diced
1 small sweet potato chunks, peeled and diced
1 tbsp medium curry paste
225 g/8 oz basmati rice
4 ripe tomatoes, peeled, deseeded and diced
600 ml/1 pint vegetable stock
175 g/6 oz cauliflower florets

50 g/2 oz peas, thawed if frozen
salt and freshly ground black pepper

To garnish:
roasted cashew nuts
raisins
fresh coriander leaves

Preheat the oven to 200°C/400°F/Gas Mark 6. Put 1 tablespoon of the vegetable oil in a large bowl with the onions and toss to coat. Lightly brush or spray a non-stick baking sheet with a little more oil. Spread half the onions on the baking sheet and cook at the top of the preheated oven for 25–30 minutes, stirring regularly, until golden and crisp. Remove from the oven and reserve for the garnish.

Meanwhile, heat a large flameproof casserole over a medium heat and add the remaining oil and onions. Cook for 5–7 minutes until softened and starting to brown. Add a little water if they start to stick. Add the garlic and ginger and cook for another minute, then add the carrot, parsnip and sweet potato. Cook the vegetables for a further 5 minutes. Add the curry paste and stir for a minute until everything is coated, then stir in the rice and tomatoes. After 2 minutes add the stock and stir well. Bring to the boil, cover and simmer over a very gentle heat for about 10 minutes.

Add the cauliflower and peas and cook for 8–10 minutes, or until the rice is tender. Season to taste with salt and pepper. Serve garnished with the crispy onions, cashew nuts, raisins and coriander.

# Brown Rice Spiced Pilaf

**SERVES 4**

1 tbsp vegetable oil
1 tbsp blanched almonds,
   flaked or chopped
1 onion, peeled
   and chopped
1 carrot, peeled and diced
225 g/8 oz flat mushrooms,
   sliced thickly
¼ tsp cinnamon

large pinch dried chilli flakes
50 g/2 oz dried apricots,
   roughly chopped
25 g/1 oz currants
zest of 1 orange
350 g/12 oz brown
   basmati rice
900 ml/1½ pints
   vegetable stock

2 tbsp freshly
   chopped coriander
2 tbsp freshly
   snipped chives
salt and freshly ground
   black pepper
snipped chives, to garnish

Preheat the oven to 200°C/400°F/Gas Mark 6. Heat the oil in a large flameproof casserole dish and add the almonds. Cook for 1–2 minutes until just browning. Be careful as the nuts will burn very easily.

Add the onion and carrot. Cook for 5 minutes until softened and starting to turn brown. Add the mushrooms and cook for a further 5 minutes, stirring often.

Add the cinnamon and chilli flakes and cook for about 30 seconds before adding the apricots, currants, orange zest and rice.

Stir together well and add the stock. Bring to the boil, cover tightly and transfer to the preheated oven. Cook for 45 minutes until the rice and vegetables are tender.

Stir the coriander and chives into the pilaf and season to taste with salt and pepper. Garnish with the extra chives and serve immediately.

*Try this:* FOR STARTERS: 36   FOR PUDDING: 362

# Baby Onion Risotto

**SERVES 4**

For the baby onions:
1 tbsp olive oil
450 g/1 lb baby onions,
    peeled and halved if large
pinch of sugar
1 tbsp freshly
    chopped thyme

For the risotto:
1 tbsp olive oil
1 small onion, peeled
    and finely chopped
2 garlic cloves, peeled
    and finely chopped
350 g/12 oz risotto rice
150 ml/¼ pint red wine
1 litre/1¾ pint hot

vegetable stock
125 g/4 oz low-fat soft
    goat's cheese
salt and freshly ground
    black pepper
sprigs of fresh thyme,
    to garnish
rocket leaves, to serve

For the baby onions, heat the olive oil in a saucepan and add the onions with the sugar. Cover and cook over a low heat, stirring occasionally, for 20–25 minutes until caramelised. Uncover during the last 10 minutes of cooking.

Meanwhile, for the risotto, heat the oil in a large frying pan and add the onion. Cook over a medium heat for 5 minutes until softened. Add the garlic and cook for a further 30 seconds.

Add the risotto rice and stir well. Add the red wine and stir constantly until the wine is almost completely absorbed by the rice. Begin adding the stock a ladleful at a time, stirring well and waiting until the last ladleful has been absorbed before stirring in the next. It will take 20–25 minutes to add all the stock by which time the rice should be just cooked but still firm. Remove from the heat.

Add the thyme to the onions and cook briefly. Increase the heat and allow the onion mixture to bubble for 2–3 minutes until almost evaporated. Add the onion mixture to the risotto along with the goat's cheese. Stir well and season to taste with salt and pepper. Garnish with sprigs of fresh thyme. Serve immediately with the rocket leaves.

*Try this:* FOR STARTERS: 68   FOR PUDDING: 372

# Spiced Couscous & Vegetables

**SERVES 4**

1 tbsp olive oil
1 large shallot, peeled
and finely chopped
1 garlic clove, peeled
and finely chopped
1 small red pepper,
deseeded and cut
into strips
1 small yellow pepper,
deseeded and cut
into strips
1 small aubergine, diced
1 tsp each turmeric, ground
cumin, ground cinnamon
and paprika
2 tsp ground coriander
large pinch saffron strands
2 tomatoes, peeled,
deseeded and diced
2 tbsp lemon juice
225 g/8 oz couscous
225 ml/8 fl oz vegetable stock
2 tbsp raisins
2 tbsp whole almonds
2 tbsp freshly
chopped parsley
2 tbsp freshly
chopped coriander
salt and freshly ground
black pepper

Heat the oil in a large frying pan and add the shallot and garlic and cook for 2–3 minutes until softened. Add the peppers and aubergine and reduce the heat.

Cook for 8–10 minutes until the vegetables are tender, adding a little water if necessary.

Test a piece of aubergine to ensure it is cooked through. Add all the spices and cook for a further minute, stirring.

Increase the heat and add the tomatoes and lemon juice. Cook for 2–3 minutes until the tomatoes have started to break down. Remove from the heat and leave to cool slightly.

Meanwhile, put the couscous into a large bowl. Bring the stock to the boil in a saucepan, then pour over the couscous. Stir well and cover with a clean tea towel.

Leave to stand for 7–8 minutes until all the stock is absorbed and the couscous is tender.

Uncover the couscous and fluff with a fork. Stir in the vegetable and spice mixture along with the raisins, almonds, parsley and coriander. Season to taste with salt and pepper and serve.

*Try this:* FOR STARTERS: 22   FOR PUDDING: 380

# Red Lentil Kedgeree
# with Avocado & Tomatoes

**SERVES 4**

150 g/5 oz basmati rice
150 g/5 oz red lentils
15 g/½ oz butter
1 tbsp sunflower oil
1 medium onion, peeled
    and chopped
1 tsp ground cumin
4 cardamom pods, bruised

1 bay leaf
450 ml/¾ pint
    vegetable stock
1 ripe avocado, peeled,
    stoned and diced
1 tbsp lemon juice
4 plum tomatoes, peeled
    and diced

2 tbsp freshly
    chopped coriander
salt and freshly ground
    black pepper
lemon or lime slices,
    to garnish

Put the rice and lentils in a sieve and rinse under cold running water. Tip into a bowl, then pour over enough cold water to cover and leave to soak for 10 minutes.

Heat the butter and oil in a saucepan. Add the sliced onion and cook gently, stirring occasionally, for 10 minutes until softened. Stir in the cumin, cardamon pods and bay leaf and cook for a further minute, stirring all the time.

Drain the rice and lentils, rinse again and add to the onions in the saucepan. Stir in the vegetable stock and bring to the boil. Reduce the heat, cover the saucepan and simmer for 14–15 minutes, or until the rice and lentils are tender.

Place the diced avocado in a bowl and toss with the lemon juice. Stir in the tomatoes and chopped coriander. Season to taste with salt and pepper.

Fluff up the rice with a fork, spoon into a warmed serving dish and spoon the avocado mixture on top. Garnish with lemon or lime slices and serve.

*Try this:* FOR STARTERS: 72  FOR PUDDING: 374

# Black Bean Chilli with Avocado Salsa

**SERVES 4**

250 g/9 oz black beans
  and black-eye beans,
  soaked overnight
2 tbsp olive oil
1 large onion, peeled
  and finely chopped
1 red pepper, deseeded
  and diced
2 garlic cloves, peeled
  and finely chopped
1 red chilli, deseeded
  and finely chopped

2 tsp chilli powder
1 tsp ground cumin
2 tsp ground coriander
400 g can chopped tomatoes
450 ml/¾ pint
  vegetable stock
1 small ripe avocado, diced
½ small red onion, peeled
  and finely chopped
2 tbsp freshly
  chopped coriander
juice of 1 lime

1 small tomato, peeled,
  deseeded and diced
salt and freshly ground
  black pepper
25 g/1 oz dark chocolate

To garnish:
half-fat crème fraîche
lime slices
sprigs of coriander

Drain the beans and place in a large saucepan with at least twice their volume of fresh water. Bring slowly to the boil, skimming off any froth that rises to the surface. Boil rapidly for 10 minutes, then reduce the heat and simmer for about 45 minutes, adding more water if necessary. Drain and reserve.

Heat the oil in a large saucepan and add the onion and pepper. Cook for 3–4 minutes until softened. Add the garlic and chilli. Cook for 5 minutes, or until the onion and pepper have softened. Add the chilli powder, cumin and coriander and cook for 30 seconds. Add the beans along with the tomatoes and stock. Bring to the boil and simmer uncovered for 40–45 minutes until the beans and vegetables are tender and the sauce has reduced.

Mix together the avocado, onion, fresh coriander, lime juice and tomato. Season with salt and pepper and set aside. Remove the chilli from the heat. Break the chocolate into pieces. Sprinkle over the chilli. Leave for 2 minutes. Stir well. Garnish with crème fraîche, lime and coriander. Serve with the avocado salsa.

*Try this:* FOR STARTERS: 76  FOR PUDDING: 360

# Boston-style Baked Beans

**SERVES 8**

| | | |
|---|---|---|
| 350 g/12 oz mixed dried pulses, e.g. haricot, flageolet, cannellini, pinto beans or chickpeas | 2 tbsp Dijon mustard | 2 medium eggs |
| | 2 tbsp light brown soft sugar | 200 ml/7 fl oz milk |
| | 125 g/4 oz plain flour | 2 tbsp melted butter |
| | 150 g/5 oz fine cornmeal | salt and freshly ground |
| 1 large onion, peeled and finely chopped | 2 tbsp caster sugar | black pepper |
| | 2½ tsp baking powder | parsley sprigs, to garnish |
| 125 g/4 oz black treacle or molasses | ½ tsp salt | |
| | 2 tbsp freshly chopped thyme | |

Preheat the oven to 130°C/250°F/Gas Mark ½. Put the pulses into a large saucepan and cover with at least twice their volume of water. Bring to the boil and simmer for 2 minutes. Leave to stand for 1 hour. Return to the boil and boil rapidly for about 10 minutes. Drain and reserve.

Mix together the onion, treacle or molasses, mustard and sugar in a large mixing bowl. Add the drained beans and 300 ml/½ pint fresh water. Stir well, bring to the boil, cover and transfer to the preheated oven for 4 hours in an ovenproof dish, stirring once every hour and adding more water if necessary.

When the beans are cooked, remove from the oven and keep warm. Increase the oven temperature to 200°C/400°F/Gas Mark 6. Mix together the plain flour, cornmeal, caster sugar, baking powder, salt and most of the thyme, reserving about one third for garnish. In a separate bowl beat the eggs, then stir in the milk and butter. Pour the wet ingredients on to the dry ones and stir just enough to combine.

Pour into a buttered 18 cm/7 inch square cake tin. Sprinkle over the remaining thyme. Bake for 30 minutes until golden and risen or until a toothpick inserted into the centre comes out clean. Cut into squares, then reheat the beans. Season to taste with salt and pepper and serve immediately, garnished with parsley sprigs.

*Try this:* FOR STARTERS: 22  FOR PUDDING: 352

# Pumpkin & Chickpea Curry

**SERVES 4**

1 tbsp vegetable oil
1 small onion, peeled
  and sliced
2 garlic cloves, peeled
  and finely chopped
2.5 cm/1 inch piece root
  ginger, peeled and grated
1 tsp ground coriander
½ tsp ground cumin
½ tsp ground turmeric

¼ tsp ground cinnamon
2 tomatoes, chopped
2 red bird's eye
  chillies, deseeded
  and finely chopped
450 g/1 lb pumpkin
  or butternut squash
  flesh, cubed
1 tbsp hot curry paste
300 ml/½ pint

vegetable stock
1 large firm banana
400 g can chickpeas, drained
  and rinsed
salt and freshly ground
  black pepper
1 tbsp freshly
  chopped coriander
coriander sprigs, to garnish
rice or naan bread, to serve

Heat 1 tablespoon of the oil in a saucepan and add the onion. Fry gently for 5 minutes until softened.

Add the garlic, ginger and spices and fry for a further minute. Add the chopped tomatoes and chillies and cook for another minute.

Add the pumpkin and curry paste and fry gently for 3–4 minutes before adding the stock. Stir well, bring to the boil and simmer for 20 minutes until the pumpkin is tender.

Thickly slice the banana and add to the pumpkin along with the chickpeas. Simmer for a further 5 minutes.

Season to taste with salt and pepper and add the chopped coriander. Serve immediately, garnished with coriander sprigs and some rice or naan bread.

*Try this:* FOR STARTERS: 42   FOR PUDDING: 378

# Roasted Butternut Squash

2 small butternut squash
4 garlic cloves, peeled
    and crushed
1 tbsp olive oil
salt and freshly ground
    black pepper
1 tbsp walnut oil
4 medium-sized leeks,
    trimmed, cleaned and

thinly sliced
1 tbsp black mustard seeds
300 g can cannellini beans,
    drained and rinsed
125 g/4 oz fine French
    beans, halved
150 ml/¼ pint
    vegetable stock
50 g/2 oz rocket

2 tbsp freshly
    snipped chives
fresh chives, to garnish

To serve:
4 tbsp low fat fromage frais
mixed salad

Preheat the oven to 200°C/400°F/Gas Mark 6. Cut the butternut squash in half lengthwise and scoop out all of the seeds.

Score the squash in a diamond pattern with a sharp knife. Mix the garlic with the olive oil and brush over the cut surfaces of the squash. Season well with salt and pepper. Put on a baking sheet and roast for 40 minutes until tender.

Heat the walnut oil in a saucepan and fry the leeks and mustard seeds for 5 minutes.

Add the drained cannellini beans, French beans and vegetable stock. Bring to the boil and simmer gently for 5 minutes until the French beans are tender.

Remove from the heat and stir in the rocket and chives. Season well. Remove the squash from the oven and allow to cool for 5 minutes. Spoon in the bean mixture. Garnish with a few snipped chives and serve immediately with the fromage frais and a mixed salad.

*Try this:* FOR STARTERS: 70   FOR PUDDING: 364

# Vegetable Cassoulet

**SERVES 6**

125 g/4 oz dried haricot
beans, soaked overnight
2 tbsp olive oil
2 garlic cloves, peeled
and chopped
225 g/8 oz baby onions,
peeled and halved
2 carrots, peeled and diced
2 celery sticks, trimmed and

finely chopped
1 red pepper, deseeded
and chopped
175 g/6 oz mixed
mushrooms, sliced
1 tbsp each freshly chopped
rosemary, thyme
and sage
150 ml/¼ pint red wine

4 tbsp tomato purée
1 tbsp dark soy sauce
salt and freshly ground
black pepper
50 g/2 oz fresh breadcrumbs
1 tbsp freshly
chopped parsley
basil sprigs, to garnish

Preheat the oven to 190°C/375°F/Gas Mark 5. Drain the haricot beans and place in a saucepan with 1.1 litres/2 pints of fresh water. Bring to the boil and boil rapidly for 10 minutes. Reduce the heat and simmer gently for 45 minutes. Drain the beans, reserving 300 ml/½ pint of the liquid.

Heat 1 tablespoon of the oil in a flameproof casserole and add the garlic, onions, carrot, celery and red pepper. Cook gently for 10–12 minutes until tender and starting to brown. Add a little water if the vegetables start to stick. Add the mushrooms and cook for a further 5 minutes until softened. Add the herbs and stir briefly.

Stir in the red wine and boil rapidly for about 5 minutes until reduced and syrupy. Stir in the reserved beans and their liquid, tomato purée and soy sauce. Season to taste with salt and pepper.

Mix together the breadcrumbs and parsley with the remaining 1 tablespoon of oil. Scatter this mixture evenly over the top of the stew. Cover loosely with foil and transfer to the preheated oven. Cook for 30 minutes. Carefully remove the foil and cook for a further 15–20 minutes until the topping is crisp and golden. Serve immediately, garnished with basil sprigs.

*Try this:* FOR STARTERS: 34   FOR PUDDING: 366

# Creamy Puy Lentils

**SERVES 4**

225 g/8 oz Puy lentils
1 tbsp olive oil
1 garlic clove, peeled and
   finely chopped
zest and juice of 1 lemon
1 tsp wholegrain mustard
1 tbsp freshly

chopped tarragon
3 tbsp half-fat crème fraîche
salt and freshly ground
   black pepper
2 small tomatoes, deseeded
   and chopped
50 g/2 oz pitted black olives

1 tbsp freshly
   chopped parsley

To garnish:
sprigs of fresh tarragon
lemon wedges

Put the lentils in a saucepan with plenty of cold water and bring to the boil. Boil rapidly for 10 minutes, reduce the heat and simmer gently for a further 20 minutes until just tender. Drain well.

Meanwhile, prepare the dressing. Heat the oil in a frying pan over a medium heat. Add the garlic and cook for about a minute until just beginning to brown. Add the lemon zest and juice.

Add the mustard and cook for a further 30 seconds. Add the tarragon and crème fraîche and season to taste with salt and pepper.

Simmer and add the drained lentils, tomatoes and olives.

Transfer to a serving dish and sprinkle the chopped parsley on top. Garnish the lentils with the tarragon sprigs and the lemon wedges and serve immediately.

*Try this:* FOR STARTERS: 72  FOR PUDDING: 380

# Mushroom Stew

**SERVES 4**

15 g/½ oz dried
  porcini mushrooms
900 g/2 lb assorted fresh
  mushrooms, wiped
2 tbsp good quality
  virgin olive oil
1 onion, peeled and
  finely chopped

2 garlic cloves, peeled and
  finely chopped
1 tbsp fresh thyme leaves
pinch of ground cloves
salt and freshly ground
  black pepper
700 g/1½ lb tomatoes,
  peeled, deseeded

  and chopped
225 g/8 oz instant polenta
600ml/1 pint vegetable stock
3 tbsp freshly chopped
  mixed herbs
sprigs of parsley,
  to garnish

Soak the porcini mushrooms in a small bowl of hot water for 20 minutes. Drain reserving the porcini mushrooms and their soaking liquor. Cut the fresh mushrooms in half and reserve.

In a saucepan, heat the oil and add the onion. Cook gently for 5–7 minutes until softened. Add the garlic, thyme and cloves and continue cooking for 2 minutes.

Add all the mushrooms and cook for 8–10 minutes until the mushrooms have softened, stirring often. Season to taste with salt and pepper and add the tomatoes and the reserved soaking liquid. Simmer, partly-covered, over a low heat for about 20 minutes until thickened. Adjust the seasoning to taste.

Meanwhile, cook the polenta according to the packet instructions using the vegetable stock. Stir in the herbs and divide between four dishes. Ladle the mushrooms over the polenta, garnish with the parsley and serve immediately.

# Huevos Rancheros

**SERVES 4**

2 tbsp olive oil
1 large onion, peeled
   and finely chopped
1 red pepper, deseeded
   and finely chopped
2 garlic cloves, peeled
   and finely chopped
2–4 green chillies, deseeded
   and finely chopped

1 tsp ground cumin
1 tsp chilli powder
2 tsp ground coriander
2 tbsp freshly
   chopped coriander
700 g/1½ lb ripe plum
   tomatoes, peeled,
   deseeded and
   roughly chopped

¼ tsp sugar
8 small eggs
4–8 flour tortillas
salt and freshly ground
   black pepper
sprigs of fresh coriander,
   to garnish
refried beans, to
   serve (optional)

Heat the oil in a large, heavy-based saucepan. Add the onion and pepper and cook over a medium heat for 10 minutes.

Add the garlic, chillies, ground cumin, chilli powder and chopped coriander and cook for a further minute. Add the tomatoes and sugar. Stir well, cover and cook gently for 20 minutes. Uncover and cook for a further 20 minutes.

Lightly poach the eggs in a large frying pan, filled with gently simmering water. Drain well and keep warm.

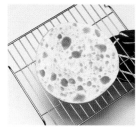

Place the tortillas briefly under a preheated hot grill. Turning once, then remove from the grill when crisp. Add the freshly chopped coriander to the tomato sauce and season to taste with salt and pepper.

To serve, arrange two tortillas on each serving plate, top with two eggs and spoon the sauce over. Garnish with sprigs of fresh coriander and serve immediately with warmed refried beans, if liked.

*Try this:* FOR STARTERS: 76   FOR PUDDING: 352

# Bulghur Wheat Salad with Minty Lemon Dressing

**SERVES 4**

125 g/4 oz bulghur wheat
10 cm /4 inch
    piece cucumber
2 shallots, peeled
125 g/4 oz baby sweetcorn
3 ripe but firm tomatoes

For the dressing:
grated rind of 1 lemon
3 tbsp lemon juice
3 tbsp freshly chopped mint
2 tbsp freshly
    chopped parsley

1–2 tsp clear honey
2 tbsp sunflower oil
salt and freshly ground
    black pepper

Place the bulghur wheat in a saucepan and cover with boiling water. Simmer for about 10 minutes, then drain thoroughly and turn into a serving bowl.

Cut the cucumber into small cubes, then chop the shallots finely and reserve. Steam the sweetcorn over a pan of boiling water for 10 minutes or until tender. Drain and slice into thick chunks.

Cut a cross on the top of each tomato and place in boiling water until their skins start to peel away. Remove the skins and the seeds and cut the tomatoes into small cubes.

Make the dressing by briskly whisking all the ingredients in a small bowl until mixed well.

When the bulghur wheat has cooled a little, add all the prepared vegetables and stir in the dressing. Season to taste with salt and pepper and serve.

# Carrot & Parsnip Terrine

**SERVES 8–10**

550 g/1¼ lb carrots, peeled
   and chopped
450 g/1 lb parsnips, peeled
   and chopped
6 tbsp half-fat crème fraîche
450 g/1 lb spinach, rinsed
1 tbsp brown sugar

1 tbsp freshly chopped parsley
½ tsp freshly grated nutmeg
salt and freshly ground
   black pepper
6 medium eggs
sprigs of fresh basil,
   to garnish

For the tomato coulis:
450 g/1 lb ripe tomatoes,
   deseeded and chopped
1 medium onion, peeled and
   finely chopped

Preheat the oven to 200°C/400°F/Gas Mark 6. Oil and line a 900 g/2 lb loaf tin with non-stick baking paper. Cook the carrots and parsnips in boiling salted water for 10–15 minutes or until very tender. Drain and purée separately. Add 2 tablespoons of crème fraîche to both the carrots and the parsnips.

Steam the spinach for 5–10 minutes or until very tender. Drain and squeeze out as much liquid as possible, then stir in the remaining crème fraîche. Add the brown sugar to the carrot purée, the parsley to the parsnip mixture and the nutmeg to the spinach. Season all to taste with salt and pepper. Beat 2 eggs, add to the spinach and turn into the prepared tin. Add another 2 beaten eggs to the carrot mixture and layer carefully on top of the spinach. Beat the remaining eggs into the parsnip purée and layer on top of the terrine.

Place the tin in a baking dish and pour in enough hot water to come halfway up the sides of the tin. Bake in the preheated oven for 1 hour until a skewer inserted into the centre comes out clean. Leave the terrine to cool for at least 30 minutes. Run a sharp knife around the edges. Turn out on to a dish and reserve.

Make the tomato coulis by simmering the tomatoes and onions together for 5–10 minutes until slightly thickened. Season to taste. Blend well in a liquidiser or food processor and serve as an accompaniment to the terrine. Garnish with sprigs of basil and serve.

*Try this:* FOR STARTERS: 70   FOR PUDDING: 376

# Chinese Salad with Soy & Ginger Dressing

**SERVES 4**

1 head of Chinese cabbage
200 g can water
    chestnuts, drained
6 spring onions, trimmed
4 ripe but firm
    cherry tomatoes
125 g/4 oz mangetout

125 g/4 oz beansprouts
2 tbsp freshly
    chopped coriander
For the soy and
    ginger dressing:
2 tbsp sunflower oil
4 tbsp light soy sauce

2.5 cm/1 inch piece root
    ginger, peeled and
    finely grated
zest and juice of 1 lemon
salt and freshly ground
    black pepper
crusty white bread, to serve

Rinse and finely shred the Chinese cabbage and place in a serving dish.

Slice the water chestnuts into small slivers and cut the spring onions diagonally into 2.5 cm/1 inch lengths, then split lengthwise into thin strips.

Cut the tomatoes in half and then slice each half into three wedges and reserve.

Simmer the mangetout in boiling water for 2 minutes until beginning to soften, drain and cut in half diagonally.

Arrange the water chestnuts, spring onions, mangetout, tomatoes and beansprouts on top of the shredded Chinese cabbage. Garnish with the freshly chopped coriander.

Make the dressing by whisking all the ingredients together in a small bowl until mixed thoroughly. Serve with the bread and the salad.

*Try this:* FOR STARTERS: 76   FOR PUDDING: 358

# Fusilli Pasta with Spicy Tomato Salsa

**SERVES 4**

6 large ripe tomatoes
2 tbsp lemon juice
2 tbsp lime juice
grated rind of 1 lime
2 shallots, peeled and

finely chopped
2 garlic cloves, peeled
and finely chopped
1–2 red chillies
1–2 green chillies

450 g/1 lb fresh fusilli pasta
4 tbsp half-fat crème fraîche
2 tbsp freshly chopped basil
sprig of oregano, to garnish

Place the tomatoes in a bowl and cover with boiling water. Allow to stand until the skins start to peel away.

Remove the skins from the tomatoes, divide each tomato in four and remove all the seeds. Chop the flesh into small dice and put in a small pan. Add the lemon and lime juice and the grated lime rind and stir well.

Add the chopped shallots and garlic. Remove the seeds carefully from the chillies, chop finely and add to the pan.

Bring to the boil and simmer gently for 5–10 minutes until the salsa has thickened slightly. Reserve the salsa to allow the flavours to develop while the pasta is cooking.

Bring a large pan of water to the boil and add the pasta. Simmer gently for 3–4 minutes or until the pasta is just tender.

Drain the pasta and rinse in boiling water. Top with a large spoonful of salsa and a small spoonful of crème fraîche. Garnish with the chopped basil and oregano and serve immediately.

*Try this:* FOR STARTERS: 66   FOR PUDDING: 378

# Hot & Spicy Red Cabbage with Apples

**SERVES 8**

900 g/2 lb red cabbage, cored and shredded
450 g/1 lb onions, peeled and finely sliced
450 g/1 lb cooking apples, peeled, cored and finely sliced

½ tsp mixed spice
1 tsp ground cinnamon
2 tbsp light soft brown sugar
salt and freshly ground black pepper
grated rind of 1 large orange
1 tbsp fresh orange juice

50 ml/2 fl oz medium sweet cider (or apple juice)
2 tbsp wine vinegar

To serve:
half-fat crème fraîche
freshly ground black pepper

Preheat the oven to 150˚C/300˚F/Gas Mark 2. Put just enough cabbage in a large casserole dish to cover the base evenly.

Place a layer of the onions and apples on top of the cabbage. Sprinkle a little of the mixed spice, cinnamon and sugar over the top. Season with salt and pepper.

Spoon over a small portion of the orange rind, orange juice and the cider. Continue to layer the casserole dish with the ingredients in the same order until used up. Pour the vinegar as evenly as possible over the top layer of the ingredients.

Cover the casserole dish with a close-fitting lid and bake in the preheated oven, stirring occasionally, for 2 hours until the cabbage is moist and tender. Serve immediately with the crème fraîche and black pepper.

 *Try this:* FOR STARTERS: 26   FOR PUDDING: 354

# Marinated Vegetable Kebabs

**SERVES 4**

2 small courgettes, cut into
   2 cm/¾ inch pieces
½ green pepper, deseeded
   and cut into 2.5 cm/
   1 inch pieces
½ red pepper, deseeded and
   cut into 2.5 cm /
   1 inch pieces
½ yellow pepper, deseeded
   and cut into 2.5 cm/
   1 inch pieces

8 baby onions, peeled
8 button mushrooms
8 cherry tomatoes
freshly chopped parsley,
   to garnish
freshly cooked couscous,
   to serve

For the marinade:
1 tbsp light olive oil
4 tbsp dry sherry
2 tbsp light soy sauce
1 red chilli, deseeded and
   finely chopped
2 garlic cloves, peeled
   and crushed
2.5 cm/1 inch piece root
   ginger, peeled and
   finely grated

Place the courgettes, peppers and baby onions in a pan of just boiled water. Bring back to the boil and simmer for about 30 seconds.

Drain and rinse the cooked vegetables in cold water and dry on absorbent kitchen paper. Thread the cooked vegetables and the mushrooms and tomatoes alternately on to skewers and place in a large shallow dish.

Make the marinade by whisking all the ingredients together until thoroughly blended. Pour the marinade evenly over the kebabs, then chill in the refrigerator for at least 1 hour. Spoon the marinade over the kebabs occasionally during this time.

Place the kebabs in a hot griddle pan or on a hot barbecue and cook gently for 10–12 minutes. Turn the kebabs frequently and brush with the marinade when needed. When the vegetables are tender, sprinkle over the chopped parsley and serve immediately with couscous.

# Cabbage Timbale

**SERVES 4-6**

1 small savoy cabbage,
    weighing about
    350 g/12 oz
salt and freshly ground
    black pepper
2 tbsp olive oil
1 leek, trimmed
    and chopped

1 garlic clove, peeled
    and crushed
75 g/3 oz long-grain rice
200 g can chopped tomatoes
300 ml/½ pint
    vegetable stock
400 g can flageolet beans,
    drained and rinsed

75 g/3 oz Cheddar
    cheese, grated
1 tbsp freshly
    chopped oregano

To garnish:
Greek yogurt with paprika
tomato wedges

Preheat the oven to 180°C/350°F/Gas Mark 4, 10 minutes before required. Remove six of the outer leaves of the cabbage. Cut off the thickest part of the stalk and blanch the leaves in lightly salted boiling water for 2 minutes. Lift out with a slotted spoon and briefly rinse under cold water and reserve.

Remove the stalks from the rest of the cabbage leaves. Shred the leaves and blanch in the boiling water for 1 minute. Drain, rinse under cold water and pat dry on absorbent kitchen paper.

Heat the oil in a frying pan and cook the leek and garlic for 5 minutes. Stir in the rice, chopped tomatoes with their juice and stock. Bring to the boil, cover and simmer for 15 minutes. Remove the lid and simmer for a further 4–5 minutes, stirring frequently, until the liquid is absorbed and the rice is tender. Stir in the flageolet beans, cheese and oregano. Season to taste with salt and pepper.

Line an oiled 1.1 litre/2 pint pudding basin with some of the large cabbage leaves, over-lapping them slightly. Fill the basin with alternate layers of rice mixture and shredded leaves, pressing down well. Cover the top with the remaining leaves. Cover with oiled tinfoil and bake in the preheated for 30 minutes. Leave to stand for 10 minutes. Turn out, cut into wedges and serve with yogurt sprinkled with paprika and tomato wedges.

*Try this:* FOR STARTERS: 42   FOR PUDDING: 376

# Chunky Vegetable & Fennel Goulash with Dumplings

**SERVES 4**

2 fennel bulbs, weighing
  about 450 g/1 lb
2 tbsp sunflower oil
1 large onion, peeled
  and sliced
1½ tbsp paprika
1 tbsp plain flour
300 ml/½ pint
  vegetable stock

400 g can chopped tomatoes
450 g/1 lb potatoes, peeled
  and cut into 2.5 cm/
  1 inch chunks
125 g/4 oz small
  button mushrooms
salt and freshly ground
  black pepper

For the dumplings:
1 tbsp sunflower oil
1 small onion, peeled and
  finely chopped
1 medium egg
3 tbsp milk
3 tbsp freshly
  chopped parsley
125 g/4 oz fresh white
  breadcrumbs

Cut the fennel bulbs in half widthways. Thickly slice the stalks and cut the bulbs into eight wedges. Heat the oil in a large saucepan or flameproof casserole. Add the onion and fennel and cook gently for 10 minutes until soft. Stir in the paprika and flour.

Remove from the heat and gradually stir in the stock. Add the chopped tomatoes, potatoes and mushrooms. Season to taste with salt and pepper. Bring to the boil, reduce the heat and simmer for 20 minutes.

Meanwhile, make the dumplings. Heat the oil in a frying pan and gently cook the onion for 10 minutes, until soft. Leave to cool for a few minutes.

In a bowl, beat the egg and milk together, then add the onion, parsley, breadcrumbs, and season to taste. With damp hands form the breadcrumb mixture into 12 round dumplings each about the size of a walnut.

Arrange the dumplings on top of the goulash. Cover and cook for a further 15 minutes, until the dumplings are cooked and the vegetables are tender. Serve immediately.

*Try this:* FOR STARTERS: 64   FOR PUDDING: 378

# Dinner Parties & Entertaining

# Seared
# Pancetta–wrapped Cod

**SERVES 4**

4 x 175 g/6 oz thick
　cod fillets
4 very thin slices of pancetta
3 tbsp capers in vinegar
1 tbsp of vegetable or
　sunflower oil

2 tbsp lemon juice
1 tbsp olive oil
freshly ground black pepper
1 tbsp freshly chopped
　parsley, to garnish

To serve:
freshly cooked vegetables
new potatoes

Wipe the cod fillets and wrap each one with the pancetta. Secure each fillet with a cocktail stick and reserve.

Drain the capers and soak in cold water for 10 minutes to remove any excess salt, then drain and reserve.

Heat the oil in a large frying pan and sear the wrapped pieces of cod fillet for about 3 minutes on each side, turning carefully with a fish slice so as not to break up the fish.

Lower the heat then continue to cook for 2–3 minutes or until the fish is cooked thoroughly.

Meanwhile, place the reserved capers, lemon juice and olive oil into a small saucepan. Grind over the black pepper.

Place the saucepan over a low heat and bring to a gentle simmer, stirring continuously for 2–3 minutes.

Once the fish is cooked, garnish with the parsley and serve with the warm caper dressing, freshly cooked vegetables and new potatoes.

# Mussels Linguine

**SERVES 4**

2 kg/4½ lb fresh mussels,
  washed and scrubbed
knob of butter
1 onion, peeled and
  finely chopped
300 ml/½ pint medium dry
  white wine

For the sauce:
1 tbsp sunflower oil
4 baby onions, peeled
  and quartered
2 garlic cloves, peeled
  and crushed
400 g can chopped tomatoes

large pinch of salt
225 g/8 oz dried linguine
  or tagliatelle
2 tbsp freshly chopped
  parsley

Soak the mussels in plenty of cold water. Leave in the refrigerator until required. When ready to use, scrub the mussel shells, removing any barnacles or beards. Discard any open mussels.

Melt the butter in a large pan. Add the mussels, onion and wine. Cover with a close-fitting lid and steam for 5–6 minutes, shaking the pan gently to ensure even cooking. Discard any mussels that have not opened, then strain and reserve the liquor.

To make the sauce, heat the oil in a medium-sized saucepan, and gently fry the quartered onion and garlic for 3–4 minutes until soft and transparent. Stir in the tomatoes and half the reserved mussel liquor. Bring to the boil and simmer for 7–10 minutes until the sauce begins to thicken.

Cook the pasta in boiling salted water for 7 minutes or or until al dente. Drain the pasta, reserving 2 tablespoons of the cooking liquor, then return the pasta and liquor to the pan.

Remove the meat from half the mussel shells. Stir into the sauce along with the remaining mussels. Pour the hot sauce over the cooked pasta and toss gently. Garnish with the parsley and serve immediately.

# Seared Tuna with Pernod & Thyme

**SERVES 4**

4 tuna or swordfish steaks
salt and freshly ground
   black pepper
3 tbsp Pernod

1 tbsp olive oil
zest and juice of 1 lime
2 tsp fresh thyme leaves
4 sun-dried tomatoes

To serve:
freshly cooked mixed rice
tossed green salad

Wipe the fish steaks with a damp cloth or dampened kitchen paper. Season both sides of the fish to taste with salt and pepper, then place in a shallow bowl and reserve.

Mix together the Pernod, olive oil, lime zest and juice with the fresh thyme leaves. Finely chop the sun-dried tomatoes and add to the Pernod mixture.

Pour the Pernod mixture over the fish and chill in the refrigerator for about 2 hours, spooning the marinade occasionally over the fish.

Heat a griddle or heavy-based frying pan. Drain the fish, reserving the marinade. Cook the fish for 3–4 minutes on each side for a steak that is still slightly pink in the middle. Or, if liked, cook the fish for 1–2 minutes longer on each side if you prefer your fish cooked through.

Place the remaining marinade in a small saucepan and bring to the boil. Pour the marinade over the fish and serve immediately, with the mixed rice and salad.

*Try this:* FOR STARTERS: 52  FOR PUDDING: 370

# Salmon with Herbed Potatoes

**SERVES 4**

450 g/1 lb baby
    new potatoes
salt and freshly ground
    black pepper
4 salmon steaks, each
    weighing about 175 g/6 oz

1 carrot, peeled and cut into
    fine strips
175 g/6 oz asparagus
    spears, trimmed
175 g/6 oz sugar snap
    peas, trimmed

finely grated rind and juice
    1 lemon
25 g/1 oz butter
4 large sprigs of fresh
    parsley

Preheat the oven to 190°C/375°F/Gas Mark 5, about 10 minutes before required.
Parboil the potatoes in lightly salted boiling water for 5–8 minutes until they are barely tender.
Drain and reserve.

Cut out four pieces of baking parchment paper, measuring 20.5 cm/8 inches square, and
place on the work surface. Arrange the parboiled potatoes on top. Wipe the salmon steaks
and place on top of the potatoes.

Place the carrot strips in a bowl with the asparagus spears, sugar snaps and grated lemon
rind and juice. Season to taste with salt and pepper. Toss lightly together.

Divide the vegetables evenly between the salmon. Dot the top of each parcel with butter and
a sprig of parsley.

To wrap a parcel, lift up two opposite sides of the paper and fold the edges together. Twist
the paper at the other two ends to seal the parcel well. Repeat with the remaining parcels.

Place the parcels on a baking tray and bake in the preheated oven for 15 minutes. Place
an unopened parcel on each plate and open just before eating.

*Try this:* FOR STARTERS: 18   FOR PUDDING: 378

# Fruits de Mer Stir Fry

**SERVES 4**

450 g/1 lb mixed fresh
   shellfish, such as tiger
   prawns, squid, scallops
   and mussels
2.5 cm/1 inch piece fresh
   root ginger
2 garlic cloves, peeled
   and crushed

2 green chillies, deseeded
   and finely chopped
3 tbsp light soy sauce
2 tbsp olive oil
200 g/7 oz baby
   sweetcorn, rinsed
200 g/7 oz asparagus tips,
   trimmed and cut in half

200 g/7 oz mangetout,
   trimmed
2 tbsp plum sauce
4 spring onions, trimmed
   and shredded, to garnish
freshly cooked rice, to serve

Prepare the shellfish. Peel the prawns and if necessary remove the thin black veins from the back of the prawns. Lightly rinse the squid rings and clean the scallops if necessary.

Remove and discard any mussels that are open. Scrub and debeard the remaining mussels, removing any barnacles from the shells. Cover the mussels with cold water until required.

Peel the root ginger and either coarsely grate or shred finely with a sharp knife and place into a small bowl. Add the garlic and chillies to the small bowl, pour in the soy sauce and mix well.

Place the mixed shellfish, except the mussels in a bowl and pour over the marinade. Stir, cover and leave for 15 minutes.

Heat a wok until hot, then add the oil and heat until almost smoking. Add the prepared vegetables, stir-fry for 3 minutes, then stir in the plum sauce.

Add the shellfish and the mussels with the marinade and stir-fry for a further 3–4 minutes, or until the fish is cooked. Discard any mussels that have not opened. Garnish with the spring onions and serve immediately with the freshly cooked rice.

*Try this:* FOR STARTERS: 46   FOR PUDDING: 368

# Fish Roulades with Rice & Spinach

**SERVES 4**

4 x 175 g/6 oz lemon
   sole, skinned
salt and freshly ground
   black pepper
1 tsp fennel seeds
75 g/3 oz long-grain

rice, cooked
150 g/5 oz white crab meat,
   fresh or canned
125 g/4 oz baby spinach,
   washed and trimmed
5 tbsp dry white wine

5 tbsp half-fat crème fraîche
2 tbsp freshly chopped
   parsley, plus extra
   to garnish
asparagus spears,
   to serve

Wipe each fish fillet with either a clean damp cloth or kitchen paper. Place on a chopping board, skinned side up and season lightly with salt and black pepper.

Place the fennel seeds in a pestle and mortar and crush lightly. Transfer to a small bowl and stir in the cooked rice. Drain the crab meat thoroughly. Add to the rice mixture and mix lightly.

Lay 2–3 spinach leaves over each fillet and top with a quarter of the crab meat mixture. Roll up and secure with a cocktail stick if necessary. Place into a large pan and pour over the wine. Cover and cook on a medium heat for 5–7 minutes or until cooked.

Remove the fish from the cooking liquor, and transfer to a serving plate and keep warm. Stir the crème fraîche into the cooking liquor and season to taste. Heat for 3 minutes, then stir in the chopped parsley.

Spoon the sauce on to the base of a plate. Cut each roulade into slices and arrange on top of the sauce. Serve with freshly cooked asparagus spears.

*Try this:* FOR STARTERS: 74   FOR PUDDING: 362

# Salmon & Filo Parcels

**SERVES 4**

1 tbsp sunflower oil
1 bunch of spring onions,
   trimmed and
   finely chopped
1 tsp paprika
175 g/6 oz long-grain
   white rice

300 ml/½ pint fish stock
salt and freshly ground
   black pepper
450 g/1 lb salmon
   fillet, cubed
1 tbsp freshly
   chopped parsley

grated rind and juice
   of 1 lemon
150 g/5 oz rocket
150 g/5 oz spinach
12 sheets filo pastry
50 g/2 oz butter, melted

Preheat the oven to 200°C/400°F/Gas Mark 6. Heat the oil in a small frying pan and gently cook the spring onions for 2 minutes. Stir in the paprika and continue to cook for 1 minute, then remove from the heat and reserve.

Put the rice in a sieve and rinse under cold running water until the water runs clear; drain. Put the rice and stock in a saucepan, bring to the boil, then cover and simmer for 10 minutes, or until the liquid is absorbed and the rice is tender. Add the spring onion mixture and fork through. Season to taste with salt and pepper, then leave to cool.

In a non-metallic bowl, mix together the salmon, parsley, lemon rind and juice and salt and pepper. Reserve. Blanch the rocket and spinach for 30 seconds in a large saucepan of boiling water, or until just wilted. Drain well in a colander and refresh in plenty of cold water, then squeeze out as much moisture as possible.

Brush three sheets of filo pastry with melted butter and lay them on top of one another. Take a quarter of the rice mixture and arrange it in an oblong in the centre of the pastry. On top of this place a quarter of the salmon followed by a quarter of the rocket and spinach.

Draw up the pastry around the filling and twist at the top to create a parcel. Repeat with the remaining pastry and filling until you have four parcels. Brush with the remaining butter. Place the parcels on a lightly oiled baking tray and cook in the preheated oven for 20 minutes, or until golden brown and cooked. Serve immediately.

*Try this:* FOR STARTERS: 56  FOR PUDDING: 368

# Mediterranean Chowder

**SERVES 6**

1 tbsp olive oil
1 tbsp butter
1 large onion, peeled and
　finely sliced
4 celery stalks, trimmed
　and thinly sliced
2 garlic cloves, peeled
　and crushed
1 bird's-eye chilli, deseeded
　and finely chopped

1 tbsp plain flour
225 g/8 oz potatoes, peeled
　and diced
600 ml/1 pint fish or
　vegetable stock
700 g/1½ lb whiting or
　cod fillet cut into 2.5 cm/
　1 inch cubes
2 tbsp freshly chopped
　parsley

125 g/4 oz large
　peeled prawns
198 g can sweetcorn,
　drained
salt and freshly ground
　black pepper
150 ml/¼ pint single cream
1 tbsp freshly snipped chives
warm, crusty bread,
　to serve

Heat the oil and butter together in a large saucepan, add the onion, celery and garlic and cook gently for 2–3 minutes until softened. Add the chilli and stir in the flour. Cook, stirring, for a further minute.

Add the potatoes to the saucepan with the stock. Bring to the boil, cover and simmer for 10 minutes. Add the fish cubes to the saucepan with the chopped parsley and cook for a further 5–10 minutes, or until the fish and potatoes are just tender.

Stir in the peeled prawns and sweetcorn and season to taste with salt and pepper. Pour in the cream and adjust the seasoning, if necessary.

Scatter the snipped chives over the top of the chowder. Ladle into six large bowls and serve immediately with plenty of warm crusty bread.

# Paella

**SERVES 6**

450 g/1 lb live mussels
4 tbsp olive oil
6 medium chicken thighs
1 medium onion, peeled and
    finely chopped
1 garlic clove, peeled
    and crushed
225 g/8 oz tomatoes,
    skinned, deseeded
    and chopped

1 red pepper, deseeded
    and chopped
1 green pepper, deseeded
    and chopped
125 g/4 oz frozen peas
1 tsp paprika
450 g/1 lb Arborio rice
½ tsp turmeric
900 ml/1½ pints chicken
    stock, warmed

175 g/6 oz large
    peeled prawns
salt and freshly ground
    black pepper
2 limes
1 lemon
1 tbsp freshly chopped basil
whole cooked unpeeled
    prawns, to garnish

Rinse the mussels under cold running water, scrubbing well to remove any grit and barnacles, then pull off the hairy 'beards'. Tap any open mussels sharply with a knife, and discard if they refuse to close. Heat the oil in a paella pan or large, heavy-based frying pan and cook the chicken thighs for 10–15 minutes until golden. Remove and keep warm.

Fry the onion and garlic in the remaining oil in the pan for 2–3 minutes, then add the tomatoes, peppers, peas and paprika and cook for a further 3 minutes. Add the rice to the pan and return the chicken with the turmeric and half the stock. Bring to the boil and simmer, gradually adding more stock as it is absorbed. Cook for 20 minutes, or until most of the stock has been absorbed and the rice is almost tender.

Put the mussels in a large saucepan with 5 cm/2 inches boiling salted water, cover and steam for 5 minutes. Discard any with shells that have not opened, then stir into the rice with the prawns. Season to taste with salt and pepper. Heat through for 2–3 minutes until piping hot. Squeeze the juice from 1 of the limes over the paella. Cut the remaining limes and the lemon into wedges and arrange on top of the paella. Sprinkle with the basil, garnish with the prawns and serve.

*Try this:* FOR STARTERS: 76  FOR PUDDING: 380

# Seafood Rice Ring

**SERVES 4**

350 g/12 oz long-grain rice
½ tsp turmeric
5 tbsp sunflower oil
2 tbsp white wine vinegar
1 tsp Dijon mustard
1 tsp caster sugar
1 tbsp mild curry paste

4 shallots, peeled and
    finely chopped
salt and freshly ground
    black pepper
125 g/4 oz peeled prawns,
    thawed if frozen
2 tbsp freshly

chopped coriander
8 fresh crevettes or large
    tiger prawns, with shells on
4 sprigs of fresh coriander,
    to garnish
lemon wedges, to serve

Lightly oil a 1.1 litre/2 pint ring mould, or line the mould with clingfilm. Cook the rice in boiling salted water with the turmeric for 15 minutes, or until tender. Drain thoroughly. Whisk 4 tablespoons of the oil with the vinegar, mustard and sugar to form a dressing and pour over the warm rice. Reserve.

Heat the remaining oil in a saucepan, add the curry paste and shallots and cook for 5 minutes, or until the shallots are just softened. Fold into the dressed rice, season to taste with salt and pepper and mix well. Leave to cool completely.

Stir in the prawns and the chopped coriander and turn into the prepared ring mould. Press the mixture down firmly with a spoon, then chill in the refrigerator for at least 1 hour.

Invert the ring onto a serving plate and fill the centre with the crevettes or tiger prawns. Arrange the cooked mussels around the edge of the ring and garnish with sprigs of fresh coriander. Serve immediately with lemon wedges.

*Try this:* FOR STARTERS: 74   FOR PUDDING: 372

# Griddled Garlic & Lemon Squid

**SERVES 4**

125 g/4 oz long-grain rice
300 ml/½ pint fish stock
225 g/8 oz squid, cleaned
finely grated rind of 1 lemon
1 garlic clove, peeled

and crushed
1 shallot, peeled and
  finely chopped
2 tbsp freshly
  chopped coriander

2 tbsp lemon juice
salt and freshly ground
  black pepper

Rinse the rice until the water runs clear, then place in a saucepan with the stock. Bring to the boil, then reduce the heat. Cover and simmer gently for 10 minutes.

Turn off the heat and leave the pan covered so the rice can steam while you cook the squid. Remove the tentacles from the squid and reserve.

Cut the body cavity in half. Using the tip of a small sharp knife, score the inside flesh of the body cavity in a diamond pattern. Do not cut all the way through.

Mix the lemon rind, crushed garlic and choppedshallot together. Place the squid in a shallow bowl and sprinkle over the lemon mixture and stir.

Heat a griddle pan until almost smoking. Cook the squid for 3–4 minutes until cooked through, then slice.

Sprinkle with the coriander and lemon juice. Season to taste with salt and pepper. Drain the rice and serve immediately with the squid.

*Try this:* FOR STARTERS: 64   FOR PUDDING: 376

# Curly Endive & Seafood Salad

**SERVES 4**

1 head of curly
   endive lettuce
2 green peppers
12.5 cm/5 inch piece
   cucumber
125 g/4 oz squid, cleaned
   and cut into thin rings
225 g/8 oz baby
   asparagus spears

125 g/4 oz smoked salmon
   slices, cut into wide strips
175 g/6 oz fresh cooked
   mussels in their shells

For the lemon dressing:
2 tbsp sunflower oil
1 tbsp white wine vinegar
5 tbsp fresh lemon juice

1–2 tsp caster sugar
1 tsp mild wholegrain
   mustard
salt and freshly ground
   black pepper

To garnish:
slices of lemon
sprigs of fresh coriander

Rinse and tear the endive into small pieces and arrange on a serving platter.

Remove the seeds from the peppers and cut the peppers and the cucumber into small dice. Sprinkle over the endive.

Bring a saucepan of water to the boil and add the squid rings. Bring the pan up to the boil again, then switch off the heat and leave it to stand for 5 minutes. Then drain and rinse thoroughly in cold water.

Cook the asparagus in boiling water for 5 minutes or until tender but just crisp. Arrange with the squid, smoked salmon and mussels on top of the salad.

To make the lemon dressing, put all the ingredients into a screw-topped jar or into a small bowl and mix thoroughly until the ingredients are combined.

Spoon 3 tablespoons of the dressing over the salad and serve the remainder in a small jug. Garnish the salad with slices of lemon and sprigs of coriander and serve.

# Pork Loin Stuffed with Orange & Hazelnut Rice

**SERVES 4**

15 g/½ oz butter
1 shallot, peeled and
    finely chopped
50 g/2 oz long-grain
    brown rice
175 ml/6 fl oz
    vegetable stock
½ orange
25 g/1 oz ready-to-eat dried

prunes, stoned
    and chopped
25 g/1 oz hazelnuts, roasted
    and roughly chopped
1 small egg, beaten
1 tbsp freshly
    chopped parsley
salt and freshly
    ground pepper

450 g/1 lb boneless pork
    tenderloin or fillet,
    trimmed

For the rice:
steamed courgettes
carrots

Preheat the oven to 190°C/375°F/Gas Mark 5, 10 minutes before required. Heat the butter in a small saucepan, add the shallot and cook gently for 2–3 minutes until softened. Add the rice and stir well for 1 minute. Add the stock, stir well and bring to the boil. Cover tightly and simmer gently for 30 minutes until the rice is tender and all the liquid is absorbed. Leave to cool.

Grate the orange rind and reserve. Remove the white pith and chop the orange flesh finely. Mix together the orange rind and flesh, prunes, hazelnuts, cooled rice, egg and parsley. Season to taste with salt and pepper.

Cut the fillet in half, then using a sharp knife, split the pork fillet lengthways almost in two, forming a pocket, leaving it just attached. Open out the pork and put between two pieces of clingfilm. Flatten using a meat mallet until about half its original thickness. Spoon the filling into the pocket and close the fillet over. Tie along the length with kitchen string at regular intervals.

Put the pork fillet in a small roasting tray and cook in the top of the preheated oven for 25–30 minutes, or until the meat is just tender. Remove from the oven and allow to rest for 5 minutes. Slice into rounds and serve with steamed courgettes and carrots.

# Crown Roast of Lamb

**SERVES 6**

1 lamb crown roast
salt and freshly ground
   black pepper
1 tbsp sunflower oil
1 small onion, peeled and
   finely chopped
2–3 garlic cloves, peeled
   and crushed

2 celery stalks, trimmed and
   finely chopped
125 g/4 oz cooked mixed
   basmati and wild rice
75 g/3 oz ready-to-eat-dried
   apricots, chopped
50 g/2 oz pine nuts, toasted
1 tbsp finely grated

orange rind
2 tbsp freshly chopped
   coriander
1 small egg, beaten
freshly roasted potatoes and
   green vegetables, to serve

Preheat the oven to 180°C/350°F/Gas Mark 4, about 10 minutes before roasting. Wipe the crown roast and season the cavity with salt and pepper. Place in a roasting tin and cover the ends of the bones with small pieces of tinfoil.

Heat the oil in a small saucepan and cook the onion, garlic and celery for 5 minutes, then remove the saucepan from the heat. Add the cooked rice with the apricots, pine nuts, orange rind and coriander. Season with salt and pepper, then stir in the egg and mix well.

Carefully spoon the prepared stuffing into the cavity of the lamb, then roast in the preheated oven for 1–1½ hours. Remove the lamb from the oven and remove and discard the tinfoil from the bones. Return to the oven and continue to cook for a further 15 minutes, or until cooked to personal preference.

Remove from the oven and leave to rest for 10 minutes before serving with the roast potatoes and freshly cooked vegetables.

*Try this:* FOR STARTERS: 54   FOR PUDDING: 378

# Teriyaki Beef

## SERVES 4

550 g/1¼ lb rump or
   sirloin steak
1 medium onion, peeled and
   finely sliced
5 cm/2 inch piece of fresh
   root ginger, peeled and
   coarsely chopped

1 bird's-eye chilli, deseeded
   and finely chopped
6 tbsp light soy sauce
2 tbsp sake or sweet sherry
1 tbsp lemon juice
1 tsp clear honey
250 g/9 oz glutinous rice

sunflower oil, for spraying

To garnish:
carrot matchsticks
daikon matchsticks
sprigs of fresh coriander

Trim the steak, discarding any fat or gristle, and place in a non-metallic shallow dish. Scatter the sliced onion over the steak. Mix the ginger with the chilli and sprinkle over the steak and onion.

Blend the soy sauce with the sake or sherry, the lemon juice and honey. Stir well, then pour over the steak and onion. Cover and leave to marinate in the refrigerator for at least 1 hour, longer if time permits. Turn the steak over, or occasionally spoon the marinade over the meat, during this time.

Place the rice in a saucepan with 450 ml/¾ pint of water and cook for 15 minutes, or until tender. Drain if necessary, then pack into 4 warmed oiled individual moulds. Quickly invert onto 4 individual warm plates and keep warm.

Spray or brush a griddle pan with oil, then heat until really hot. Drain the steak and cook in the griddle pan for 2–3 minutes on each side, or until cooked to personal preference. Remove from the pan and slice thinly. Arrange on the warm serving plates, garnish with the carrot and daikon matchsticks and coriander sprigs, then serve.

# Chilli Roast Chicken

## SERVES 4

3 medium-hot fresh red
  chillies, deseeded
½ tsp ground turmeric
1 tsp cumin seeds
1 tsp coriander seeds
2 garlic cloves, peeled
  and crushed
2.5 cm/1 inch piece fresh
  root ginger, peeled

  and chopped
1 tbsp lemon juice
1 tbsp olive oil
2 tbsp roughly chopped
  fresh coriander
½ tsp salt
freshly ground black pepper
1.4 kg/3 lb oven-ready
  chicken

15 g/½ oz unsalted
  butter, melted
550 g/1¼ lb butternut squash
fresh parsley and coriander
  sprigs, to garnish

To serve:
4 baked potatoes
seasonal green vegetables

Preheat the oven to 190°C/375°F/Gas Mark 5. Roughly chop the chillies and put in a food processor with the turmeric, cumin seeds, coriander seeds, garlic, ginger, lemon juice, olive oil, coriander, salt, pepper and 2 tablespoons of cold water. Blend to a paste, leaving the ingredients still slightly chunky.

Starting at the neck end of the chicken, gently ease up the skin to loosen it from the breast. Reserve 3 tablespoons of the paste. Push the remaining paste over the chicken breast under the skin, spreading it evenly.

Put the chicken in a large roasting tin. Mix the reserved chilli paste with the melted butter. Use 1 tablespoon to brush evenly over the chicken, roast in the preheated oven for 20 minutes. Meanwhile, halve, peel and scoop out the seeds from the butternut squash. Cut into large chunks and mix in the remaining chilli paste and butter mixture.

Arrange the butternut squash around the chicken. Roast for a further hour, basting with the cooking juices about every 20 minutes until the chicken is fully cooked and the squash tender. Garnish with parsley and coriander. Serve hot with baked potatoes and green vegetables.

*Try this:* FOR STARTERS: 46  FOR PUDDING: 352

# Stir–fried Chicken with Spinach, Tomatoes & Pine Nuts

**SERVES 4**

50 g/2 oz pine nuts
2 tbsp sunflower oil
1 red onion, peeled and
  finely chopped
450 g/1 lb skinless, boneless
  chicken breast fillets,
  cut into strips

450 g/1 lb cherry
  tomatoes, halved
225 g/8 oz baby
  spinach, washed
salt and freshly ground
  black pepper
¼ tsp freshly

grated nutmeg
2 tbsp balsamic vinegar
50 g/2 oz raisins
freshly cooked ribbon
  noodles tossed in butter,
  to serve

Heat the wok and add the pine nuts. Dry-fry for about 2 minutes, shaking often to ensure that they toast but do not burn. Remove and reserve. Wipe any dust from the wok.

Heat the wok again, add the oil and when hot, add the red onion and stir-fry for 2 minutes. Add the chicken and stir-fry for 2–3 minutes, or until golden brown. Reduce the heat, toss in the cherry tomatoes and stir-fry gently until the tomatoes start to disintegrate.

Add the baby spinach and stir-fry for 2–3 minutes, or until they start to wilt. Season to taste with salt and pepper, then sprinkle in the grated nutmeg and drizzle in the balsamic vinegar. Finally, stir in the raisins and reserved toasted pine nuts. Serve immediately on a bed of buttered ribbon noodles.

*Try this:* FOR STARTERS: 36  FOR PUDDING: 378

# Sauvignon Chicken & Mushroom Filo Pie

**SERVES 4**

1 onion, peeled
  and chopped
1 leek, trimmed
  and chopped
225 ml/8 fl oz chicken stock
3 x 175 g/6 oz
  chicken breasts
150 ml/¼ pint dry
  white wine

1 bay leaf
175 g/6 oz baby
  button mushrooms
2 tbsp plain flour
1 tbsp freshly
  chopped tarragon
salt and freshly ground
  black pepper
sprig of fresh parsley,

to garnish
seasonal vegetables,
  to serve

For the topping:
75 g/3 oz (about 5 sheets)
  filo pastry
1 tbsp sunflower oil
1 tsp sesame seeds

Preheat the oven to 190˚C/375˚F/Gas Mark 5. Put the onion and leek in a heavy-based saucepan with 125 ml/4 fl oz of the stock. Bring to the boil, cover and simmer for 5 minutes, then uncover and cook until all the stock has evaporated and the vegetables are tender.

Cut the chicken into bite-sized cubes. Add to the pan with the remaining stock, wine and bay leaf. Cover and gently simmer for 5 minutes. Add the mushrooms and simmer for a further 5 minutes.

Blend the flour with 3 tablespoons of cold water. Stir into the pan and cook, stirring all the time until the sauce has thickened. Stir the tarragon into the sauce and season with salt and pepper. Spoon the mixture into a 1.2 litre/2 pint pie dish, discarding the bay leaf.

Lightly brush a sheet of filo pastry with a little of the oil. Crumple the pastry slightly. Arrange on top of the filling. Repeat with the remaining filo sheets and oil, then sprinkle the top of the pie with the sesame seeds.

Bake the pie on the middle shelf of the preheated oven for 20 minutes until the filo pastry topping is golden and crisp. Garnish with a sprig of parsley. Serve the pie immediately with the seasonal vegetables.

*Try this:* FOR STARTERS: 40  FOR PUDDING: 376

# Poached Chicken with Salsa Verde Herb Sauce

**SERVES 6**

6 boneless chicken breasts,
  each about 175 g /6 oz
600 ml/1 pint chicken stock,
  preferably homemade

For the salsa verde:
2 garlic cloves, peeled
  and chopped
4 tbsp freshly chopped
  parsley

3 tbsp freshly chopped mint
2 tsp capers
2 tbsp chopped gherkins
  (optional)
2–3 anchovy fillets in olive
  oil, drained and finely
  chopped (optional)
1 handful wild rocket leaves,
  chopped (optional)
2 tbsp lemon juice or red

wine vinegar
125 ml/4 fl oz extra virgin
  olive oil
salt and freshly ground
  black pepper
sprigs of mint, to garnish
freshly cooked vegetables,
  to serve

Place the chicken breasts with the stock in a large frying pan and bring to the boil. Reduce the heat and simmer for 10–15 minutes, or until cooked. Leave to cool in the stock.

To make the salsa verde, switch the motor on a food processor, then drop in the garlic cloves and chop finely. Add the parsley and mint and, using the pulse button, pulse 2–3 times. Add the capers and, if using, add the gherkins, anchovies and rocket. Pulse 2–3 times until the sauce is evenly textured.

With the machine still running, pour in the lemon juice or red wine vinegar, then add the olive oil in a slow, steady stream until the sauce is smooth. Season to taste with salt and pepper, then transfer to a large serving bowl and reserve.

Carve each chicken breast into thick slices and arrange on serving plates, fanning out the slices slightly. Spoon over a little of the salsa verde on to each chicken breast, garnish with sprigs of mint and serve immediately with freshly cooked vegetables.

 *Try this:* FOR STARTERS: 52   FOR PUDDING: 358

# Teriyaki Turkey with Oriental Vegetables

**SERVES 4**

1 red chilli
1 garlic clove, peeled
  and crushed
2.5 cm/1 inch piece root
  ginger, peeled and grated
3 tbsp dark soy sauce
1 tsp sunflower oil
350 g/12 oz skinless,
  boneless turkey breast

1 tbsp sesame oil
1 tbsp sesame seeds
2 carrots, peeled and cut
  into matchstick strips
1 leek, trimmed
  and shredded
125 g/4 oz broccoli, cut into
  tiny florets
1 tsp cornflour

3 tbsp dry sherry
125 g/4 oz mangetout, cut
  into thin strips

To serve:
freshly cooked egg noodles
sprinkling of sesame seeds

Halve, deseed and thinly slice the chilli. Put into a small bowl with the garlic, ginger, soy sauce and sunflower oil. Cut the turkey into thin strips. Add to the mixture and mix until well coated. Cover with clingfilm and marinate in the refrigerator for at least 30 minutes.

Heat a wok or large frying pan. Add 2 teaspoons of the sesame oil. When hot, remove the turkey from the marinade. Stir-fry for 2–3 minutes until browned and cooked. Remove from the pan and reserve.

Heat the remaining 1 teaspoon of oil in the wok. Add the sesame seeds and stir-fry for a few seconds until they start to change colour. Add the carrots, leek and broccoli and continue stir-frying for 2–3 minutes.

Blend the cornflour with 1 tablespoon of cold water to make a smooth paste. Stir in the sherry and marinade. Add to the wok with the mangetout and cook for 1 minute, stirring all the time until thickened. Return the turkey to the pan and continue cooking for 1–2 minutes or until the turkey is hot, the vegetables are tender and the sauce is bubbling. Serve the turkey and vegetables immediately with the egg noodles. Sprinkle with the sesame seeds.

*Try this:* FOR STARTERS: 52   FOR PUDDING: 358

# Turkey Escalopes Marsala with Wilted Watercress

**SERVES 4**

| | | |
|---|---|---|
| 4 turkey escalopes, each about 150 g/5 oz | black pepper | wiped and quartered |
| 25 g/1 oz plain flour | 1–2 tbsp olive oil | 50 ml/2 fl oz dry |
| ½ tsp dried thyme | 125 g/4 oz watercress | Marsala wine |
| salt and freshly ground | 40 g/1½ oz butter | 50 ml/2 fl oz chicken |
| | 225 g/8 oz mushrooms, | stock or water |

Place each turkey escalope between 2 sheets of non-stick baking parchment and using a meat mallet or rolling pin pound to make an escalope about 3 mm/⅛ inch thick. Put the flour in a shallow dish, add the thyme, season to taste with salt and pepper and stir to blend. Coat each escalope lightly on both sides with the flour mixture, then reserve.

Heat the olive oil in a large frying pan, then add the watercress and stir-fry for about 2 minutes, until just wilted and brightly coloured. Season with salt and pepper. Using a slotted spoon, transfer the watercress to a plate and keep warm.

Add half the butter to the frying pan and when melted, add the mushrooms. Stir-fry for 4 minutes, or until golden and tender. Remove from the pan and reserve. Add the remaining butter to the pan and, working in batches if necessary, cook the flour-coated escalopes for 2–3 minutes on each side, or until golden and cooked thoroughly, adding the remaining oil, if necessary. Remove from the pan and keep warm.

Add the Marsala wine to the pan and stir, scraping up any browned bits from the bottom of the pan. Add the stock or water and bring to the boil over a high heat. Season lightly. Return the escalopes and mushrooms to the pan and reheat gently until piping hot. Divide the warm watercress between four serving plates. Arrange one escalope over each serving of wilted watercress and spoon over the mushrooms and Marsala sauce. Serve immediately.

*Try this:* FOR STARTERS: 58   FOR PUDDING: 366

# Guinea Fowl with Calvados & Apples

**SERVES 4**

4 guinea fowl supremes,
  each about 150 g/5 oz,
  skinned
1 tbsp plain flour
1 tbsp sunflower oil
1 onion, peeled and
  finely sliced
1 garlic clove, peeled

  and crushed
1 tsp freshly chopped thyme
150 ml/¼ pint dry cider
salt and freshly ground
  black pepper
3 tbsp Calvados brandy
sprigs of fresh thyme,
  to garnish

For the caramelised apples:
15 g/½ oz unsalted butter
2 red-skinned eating
  apples, quartered,
  cored and sliced
1 tsp caster sugar

Lightly dust the guinea fowl supremes with the flour. Heat 2 teaspoons of the oil in a large non-stick frying pan and cook the supremes for 2–3 minutes on each side until browned. Remove from the pan and reserve.

Heat the remaining teaspoon of oil in the pan and add the onion and garlic. Cook over a medium heat for 10 minutes, stirring occasionally until soft and just beginning to colour. Stir in the chopped thyme and cider. Return the guinea fowl to the pan, season with salt and pepper and bring to a very gentle simmer. Cover and cook over a low heat for 15–20 minutes or until the guinea fowl is tender. Remove the guinea fowl and keep warm. Turn up the heat and boil the sauce until thickened and reduced by half.

Meanwhile, prepare the caramelised apples. Melt the butter in a small, non-stick pan, add the apple slices in a single layer and sprinkle with the sugar. Cook until the apples are tender and beginning to caramelise, turning once. Put the Calvados in a metal ladle or small saucepan and gently heat until warm. Carefully set alight with a match, let the flames die down, then stir into the sauce.

Serve the guinea fowl with the sauce spooned over and garnished with the caramelised apples and sprigs of fresh thyme.

*Try this:* FOR STARTERS: 26   FOR PUDDING: 370

# Duck with Berry Sauce

**SERVES 4**

4 x 175 g/6 oz boneless
    duck breasts
salt and freshly ground
    black pepper
1 tsp sunflower oil

For the sauce:
juice of 1 orange

1 bay leaf
3 tbsp redcurrant jelly
150 g/5 oz fresh or frozen
    mixed berries
2 tbsp dried cranberries
    or cherries
½ tsp soft light brown sugar
1 tbsp balsamic vinegar

1 tsp freshly chopped mint
sprigs of fresh mint,
    to garnish

To serve:
freshly cooked potatoes
freshly cooked green beans

Remove the skins from the duck breasts and season with a little salt and pepper. Brush a griddle pan with the oil, then heat on the stove until smoking hot.

Place the duck, skinned-side down in the pan. Cook over a medium-high heat for 5 minutes, or until well browned. Turn the duck and cook for 2 minutes. Lower the heat and cook for a further 5–8 minutes, or until cooked, but still slightly pink in the centre. Remove from the pan and keep warm.

While the duck is cooking, make the sauce. Put the orange juice, bay leaf, redcurrant jelly, fresh or frozen and dried berries and sugar in a small griddle pan. Add any juices left in the griddle pan to the small pan. Slowly bring to the boil, lower the heat and simmer uncovered for 4–5 minutes, until the fruit is soft.

Remove the bay leaf. Stir in the vinegar and chopped mint and season to taste with salt and pepper.

Slice the duck breasts on the diagonal and arrange on serving plates. Spoon over the berry sauce and garnish with sprigs of fresh mint. Serve immediately with the potatoes and green beans.

# Sticky–glazed Spatchcocked Poussins

**SERVES 4**

2 poussins, each about
  700 g/1½ lb
salt and freshly ground
  black pepper
4 kumquats, thinly sliced
assorted salad leaves,
  crusty bread or new

potatoes, to serve

For the glaze:
zest of 1 small lemon,
  finely grated
1 tbsp lemon juice
1 tbsp dry sherry

2 tbsp clear honey
2 tbsp dark soy sauce
2 tbsp wholegrain mustard
1 tsp tomato purée
½ tsp Chinese five
  spice powder

Preheat the grill just before cooking. Place one of the poussins breast-side down on a board. Using poultry shears, cut down one side of the backbone. Cut down the other side of the backbone. Remove the bone. Open out the poussin and press down hard on the breast bone with the heel of your hand to break it and to flatten the poussin.

Thread two skewers crosswise through the bird to keep it flat, ensuring that each skewer goes through a wing and out through the leg on the opposite side. Repeat with the other bird. Season both sides of the bird with salt and pepper.

To make the glaze, mix together the lemon zest and juice, sherry, honey, soy sauce, mustard, tomato purée and Chinese five-spice powder and use to brush all over the poussins.

Place the poussins skin-side down on a grill rack and grill under a medium heat for 15 minutes, brushing halfway through with more glaze. Turn the poussins over and grill for 10 minutes. Brush again with glaze and arrange the kumquat slices on top. Grill for a further 15 minutes until well-browned and cooked through. If they start to brown too quickly, turn the grill down.

Remove the skewers and cut each poussin in half along the breastbone. Serve immediately with the salad, crusty bread or new potatoes.

*Try this:* FOR STARTERS: 42   FOR PUDDING: 368

# Fruity Rice–stuffed Poussins

**SERVES 6**

For the rice stuffing:
225 ml/8 fl oz port
125 g/4 oz raisins
125 g/4 oz ready-to-eat dried apricots, chopped
2 tbsp olive oil
1 medium onion, peeled and finely chopped
1 celery stalk, trimmed and finely sliced
2 garlic cloves, peeled and finely chopped
1½ tsp mixed spice

1 tsp each dried oregano and mint or basil
225 g/8 oz unsweetened canned chestnuts, chopped
200 g/7 oz long-grain white rice, cooked
grated rind and juice of 2 oranges
350 ml/12 fl oz chicken stock
50 g/2 oz walnut halves, lightly toasted and chopped

2 tbsp each freshly chopped mint and parsley
salt and freshly ground black pepper

6 oven-ready poussins
50 g/2 oz butter, melted

To garnish:
fresh herbs
orange wedges

Preheat the oven to 180°C/350°F/Gas Mark 4. To make the stuffing, place the port, raisins and apricots in a bowl and leave for 15 minutes. Heat the oil in a large saucepan. Add the onion and celery and cook for 3–4 minutes. Add the garlic, mixed spice, herbs and chestnuts and cook for 4 minutes, stirring occasionally. Add the rice, half the orange rind and juice and the stock. Simmer for 5 minutes until most liquid is absorbed.

Drain the raisins and apricots, reserving the port. Stir into the rice with the walnuts, mint, parsley and seasoning and cook for 2 minutes. Remove and cool.

Rinse the poussin cavities, pat dry and season with salt and pepper. Lightly fill the cavities with the stuffing. Tie the legs of together, tucking in the tail. Form any extra stuffing into balls.

Place in roasting tins with stuffing balls and brush with melted butter. Drizzle over the remaining butter, remaining orange rind and juice and port. Roast in the preheated oven for 50 minutes or until golden and cooked, basting every 15 minutes. Transfer to a platter, cover with tinfoil and rest. Pour over any pan juices. Garnish with herbs and orange wedges. Serve with the stuffing.

*Try this:* FOR STARTERS: 54   FOR PUDDING: 366

# Chargrilled Vegetable & Goats' Cheese Pizza

**SERVES 4**

125 g/4 oz baking potato
1 tbsp olive oil
225 g/8 oz strong white flour
½ tsp salt
1 tsp easy-blend dried yeast

For the topping:
1 medium aubergine,
  thinly sliced
2 small courgettes, trimmed
and sliced lengthways
1 yellow pepper, quartered
  and deseeded
1 red onion, peeled
  and sliced into very
  thin wedges
5 tbsp olive oil
175 g/6 oz cooked new
  potatoes, halved
400 g can chopped
tomatoes, drained
2 tsp freshly
  chopped oregano
125 g/4 oz mozzarella
  cheese, cut into
  small cubes
125 g/4 oz goats'
  cheese, crumbled

Preheat the oven to 220°C/425°F/Gas Mark 7, 15 minutes before baking. Put a baking sheet in the oven to heat up. Cook the potato in lightly salted boiling water until tender. Peel and mash with the olive oil until smooth.

Sift the flour and salt into a bowl. Stir in the yeast. Add the mashed potato and 150 ml/ ¼ pint warm water and mix to a soft dough. Knead for 5–6 minutes, until smooth. Put the dough in a bowl, cover with clingfilm and leave to rise in a warm place for 30 minutes.

To make the topping, arrange the aubergine, courgettes, pepper and onion, skin-side up, on a grill rack and brush with 4 tablespoons of the oil. Grill for 4–5 minutes. Turn the vegetables and brush with the remaining oil. Grill for 3–4 minutes. Cool, skin and slice the pepper. Put all of the vegetables in a bowl, add the halved new potatoes and toss gently together. Set aside.

Briefly re-knead the dough then roll out to a 30.5–35.5 cm/12–14 inch round, according to preferred thickness. Mix the tomatoes and oregano together and spread over the pizza base. Scatter over the mozzarella cheese. Put the pizza on the preheated baking sheet and bake for 8 minutes. Arrange the vegetables and goats' cheese on top and bake for 8–10 minutes. Serve.

# Puddings & Desserts

# Orange Freeze

**SERVES 4**

4 large oranges
about 300 ml/½ pint low-fat
   vanilla ice cream
225 g/8 oz raspberries

75 g/3 oz icing sugar, sifted
redcurrant sprigs,
   to decorate

Set the freezer to rapid freeze. Using a sharp knife carefully cut the lid off each orange. Scoop out the flesh from the orange, discarding any pips and thick pith. Place the shells and lids in the freezer and chop any remaining orange flesh.

Whisk together the orange juice, orange flesh and vanilla ice cream, until well blended. Cover and freeze, for about 2 hours, occasionally breaking up the ice crystals with a fork or a whisk. Stir the mixture from around the edge of the container into the centre, then level and return to the freezer. Do this 2–3 times then leave until almost frozen solid.

Place a large scoop of the ice cream mixture into the frozen shells. Add another scoop on top, so that there is plenty outside of the orange shell and return to the freezer for 1 hour.

Arrange the lids on top and freeze for a further 2 hours, until the filled orange shell is completely frozen solid.

Meanwhile, using a nylon sieve press the raspberries into a bowl using the back of a wooden spoon and mix together with the icing sugar. Spoon the raspberry coulis on to four serving plates and place an orange at the centre of each. Dust with icing sugar and serve decorated with the redcurrants. Remember to return the freezer to its normal setting.

# Rice Pudding

**SERVES 4**

60 g/2½ oz pudding rice
50 g/2 oz granulated sugar
410 g can light
    evaporated milk

300 ml/½ pint semi-
    skimmed milk
pinch of freshly
    grated nutmeg

25 g/1 oz half-fat butter
reduced sugar jam,
    to decorate

Preheat the oven to 150°C/300°F/Gas Mark 2. Lightly oil a large ovenproof dish. Sprinkle the rice and the sugar into the dish and mix.

Bring the evaporated milk and milk to the boil in a small pan, stirring occasionally. Stir the milks into the rice and mix well until the rice is coated thoroughly. Sprinkle over the nutmeg, cover with tinfoil and bake in the preheated oven for 30 minutes.

Remove the pudding from the oven and stir well, breaking up any lumps. Cover with the same tinfoil. Bake in the preheated oven for a further 30 minutes. Remove from the oven and stir well again.

Dot the pudding with butter and bake for a further 45–60 minutes, until the rice is tender and the skin is browned. Divide the pudding into four individual serving bowls. Top with a large spoonful of the jam and serve immediately.

# Orange Curd & Plum Puddings

**SERVES 4**

700 g/1½lb plums, stoned
    and quartered
2 tbsp light brown sugar
grated rind of ½ lemon
25 g/1 oz butter, melted

1 tbsp olive oil
6 sheets filo pastry
½ x 411 g jar luxury
    orange curd
50 g/2 oz sultanas

icing sugar, to decorate
half-fat thick set Greek
    yogurt, to serve

Preheat the oven to 200°C/400° F/Gas Mark 6. Lightly oil a 20.5 cm/8 inch round cake tin.
Cook the plums with 2 tablespoons of the light brown sugar for 8–10 minutes to soften them,
remove from the heat and reserve.

Mix together the lemon rind, butter and oil. Lay a sheet of pastry in the prepared cake tin and
brush with the lemon rind mixture.

Cut the sheets of filo pastry in half and then place one half sheet in the cake tin and brush again.
Top with the remaining halved sheets of pastry brushing each time with the lemon rind
mixture. Fold each sheet in half lengthwise to line the sides of the tin to make a filo case.

Mix together the plums, orange curd and sultanas and spoon into the pastry case. Draw the
pastry edges up over the filling to enclose. Brush the remaining sheets of filo pastry with the
lemon rind mixture and cut into thick strips.

Scrunch each strip of pastry and arrange on top of the pie. Bake in the preheated oven for
25 minutes, until golden. Sprinkle with icing sugar and serve with the Greek yogurt.

# Sweet–stewed Dried Fruits

**SERVES 4**

500 g/1 lb 2 oz packet mixed
   dried fruit salad
450 ml/¾ pint apple juice
2 tbsp clear honey

2 tbsp brandy
1 lemon
1 orange

To decorate:
half-fat crème fraîche
fine strips of pared
   orange rind

Place the fruits, apple juice, clear honey and brandy in a small saucepan.

Using a small, sharp knife or a zester, carefully remove the zest from the lemon and orange and place in the pan. Squeeze the juice from the lemon and oranges and add to the pan.

Bring the fruit mixture to the boil and simmer for about 1 minute. Remove the pan from the heat and allow the mixture to cool completely.

Transfer the mixture to a large bowl, cover with clingfilm and chill in the refrigerator overnight to allow the flavours to blend.

Spoon the stewed fruit in four shallow dessert dishes. Decorate with a large spoonful of half-fat crème fraîche and a few strips of the pared orange rind and serve.

*Try this:* FOR STARTERS: 30  FOR MAIN MEAL: 170

# Autumn Fruit Layer

**SERVES 4**

450 g/1 lb Bramley
  cooking apples
225 g/8 oz blackberries
50 g/2 oz soft brown sugar
juice of 1 lemon

50 g/2 oz low-fat spread
200 g/7 oz breadcrumbs
225 g/8 oz honey-coated nut
  mix, chopped
redcurrants and mint leaves,

to decorate
half-fat whipped cream or
  reduced-fat ice cream,
to serve

Peel, core and slice the cooking apples and place in a saucepan with the blackberries, sugar and lemon juice.

Cover the fruit mixture and simmer, stirring occasionally for about 15 minutes or until the apples and blackberries have formed into a thick purée. Remove the pan from the heat and allow to cool.

Melt the low-fat spread in a frying pan and cook the breadcrumbs for 5–10 minutes, stirring occasionally until golden and crisp. Remove the pan from the heat and stir in the nuts. Allow to cool.

Alternately layer the fruit purée and breadcrumbs into four tall glasses. Store the desserts in the refrigerator to chill and remove when ready to serve.

Decorate with redcurrants and mint leaves and serve with half-fat whipped cream or a reduced-fat vanilla or raspberry ice cream.

*Try this:* FOR STARTERS: 40   FOR MAIN MEAL: 172

# Oaty Fruit Puddings

**SERVES 4**

125 g/4 oz rolled oats
50 g/2 oz low-fat
  spread, melted
2 tbsp chopped almonds
1 tbsp clear honey

pinch of ground cinnamon
2 pears, peeled, cored and
  finely chopped
1 tbsp marmalade
orange zest, to decorate

low-fat custard or fruit-
  flavoured low-fat yogurt,
  to serve

Preheat the oven to 200°C/400°F/Gas Mark 6. Lightly oil and line the bases of four individual pudding bowls or muffin tins with a small circle of greaseproof paper.

Mix together the oats, low-fat spread, nuts, honey and cinnamon in a small bowl. Using a spoon, spread two thirds of the oaty mixture over the base and around the sides of the pudding bowls or muffin tins.

Toss together the pears and marmalade and spoon into the oaty cases. Scatter over the remaining oaty mixture to cover the pears and marmalade.

Bake in the preheated oven for 15–20 minutes, until cooked and the tops of the puddings are golden and crisp.

Leave for 5 minutes before removing the pudding bowls or the muffin tins. Decorate with orange zest and serve hot with low-fat custard or low-fat fruit-flavoured yogurt.

*Try this:* FOR STARTERS: 32  FOR MAIN MEAL: 146

# Fruit Salad

**SERVES 4**

125 g/4 oz caster sugar
3 oranges
700 g/1½ lb lychees,
   peeled and stoned
1 small mango
1 small pineapple
1 papaya

4 pieces stem ginger
   in syrup
4 tbsp stem ginger syrup
125 g/4 oz Cape
   gooseberries
125 g/4 oz strawberries,
   hulled

½ tsp almond essence

To decorate:
lime zest
mint leaves

Place the sugar and 300 ml/½ pint of water in a small pan and heat, gently stirring until the sugar has dissolved. Bring to the boil and simmer for 2 minutes. Once a syrup has formed, remove from the heat and allow to cool.

Using a sharp knife, cut away the skin from the oranges, then slice thickly. Cut each slice in half and place in a serving dish with the syrup and lychees.

Peel the mango, then cut into thick slices around each side of the stone. Discard the stone and cut the slices into bite-sized pieces and add to the syrup.

Using a sharp knife again, carefully cut away the skin from the pineapple. Remove the central core using the knife or an apple corer, then cut the pineapple into segments and add to the syrup.

Peel the papaya, then cut in half and remove the seeds. Cut the flesh into chunks, slice the ginger into matchsticks and add with the ginger syrup to the fruit in the syrup.

Prepare the Cape gooseberries, by removing the thin, papery skins and rinsing lightly. Halve the strawberries, add to the fruit with the almond essence and chill for 30 minutes. Scatter with mint leaves and lime zest to decorate and serve.

# Summer Pavlova

**SERVES 6–8**

4 medium egg whites
225 g/8 oz caster sugar
1 tsp vanilla essence
2 tsp white wine vinegar
1½ tsp cornflour

300 ml/½ pint half-fat
   Greek-set yogurt
2 tbsp honey
225 g/8 oz strawberries,
   hulled

125 g/4 oz raspberries
125 g/4 oz blueberries
4 kiwis, peeled and sliced
icing sugar, to decorate

Preheat the oven to 150°C/300°F/Gas Mark 2. Line a baking sheet with a sheet of greaseproof or baking parchment paper.

Place the egg whites in a clean grease-free bowl and whisk until very stiff. Whisk in half the sugar, vanilla essence, vinegar and cornflour, continue whisking until stiff. Gradually, whisk in the remaining sugar, a teaspoonful at a time until very stiff and glossy.

Using a large spoon, arrange spoonfuls of the meringue in a circle on the greaseproof paper or baking parchment paper.

Bake in the preheated oven for 1 hour until crisp and dry. Turn the oven off and leave the meringue in the oven to cool completely.

Remove the meringue from the baking sheet and peel away the parchment paper. Mix together the yogurt and honey. Place the pavlova on a serving plate and spoon the yogurt into the centre.

Scatter over the strawberries, raspberries, blueberries and kiwis. Dust with the icing sugar and serve.

*Try this:* FOR STARTERS: 34   FOR MAIN MEAL: 168

# Poached Pears

**SERVES 4**

2 small cinnamon sticks
125 g/4 oz caster sugar
300 ml/½ pint red wine
150 ml/¼ pint water

thinly pared rind and juice of
1 small orange
4 firm pears
orange slices,

to decorate
frozen vanilla yogurt,
or low-fat ice cream,
to serve

Place the cinnamon sticks on the work surface and with a rolling pin, slowly roll down the side of the cinnamon stick to bruise. Place in a large heavy-based saucepan.

Add the sugar, wine, water, pared orange rind and juice to the pan and bring slowly to the boil, stirring occasionally, until the sugar is dissolved.

Meanwhile peel the pears, leaving the stalks on. Cut out the cores from the bottom of the pears and level them so that they stand upright.

Stand the pears in the syrup, cover the pan and simmer for 20 minutes or until tender. Remove the pan from the heat and leave the pears to cool in the syrup, turning occasionally.

Arrange the pears on serving plates and spoon over the syrup. Decorate with the orange slices and serve with the yogurt or low-fat ice cream and any remaining juices.

*Try this:* FOR STARTERS: 36   FOR MAIN MEAL: 174

# Grape & Almond Layer

**SERVES 4**

300 ml/½ pint low-fat
   fromage frais
300 ml/½ pint half-fat
   Greek-set yogurt
3 tbsp icing sugar, sifted

2 tbsp crème de cassis
450 g/1 lb red grapes
175 g/6 oz Amaretti biscuits
2 ripe passion fruit

To decorate:
icing sugar
extra grapes, optional

Mix together the fromage frais and yogurt in a bowl and lightly fold in the sifted icing sugar and crème de cassis with a large metal spoon or rubber spatula until lightly blended.

Using a small knife, remove the seeds from the grapes if necessary. Rinse lightly and pat dry on absorbent kitchen paper.

Place the deseeded grapes in a bowl and stir in any juice from the grapes from deseeding.

Place the Amaretti biscuits in a polythene bag and crush roughly with a rolling pin. Alternatively, use a food processor.

Cut the passion fruit in half, scoop out the seeds with a teaspoon and reserve.

Divide the yogurt mixture between four tall glasses, then layer alternately with grapes, crushed biscuits and most of the passion fruit seeds. Top with the yogurt mixture and the remaining passion fruit seeds. Chill for 1 hour and decorate with extra grapes. Lightly dust with icing sugar and serve.

# Summary Pudding

**SERVES 4**

450 g/1 lb redcurrants
125 g/4 oz caster sugar
350 g/12 oz strawberries,
   hulled and halved
125 g/4 oz raspberries

2 tbsp Grand Marnier
   or Cointreau
8–10 medium slices white
   bread, crusts removed
mint sprigs, to decorate

low-fat Greek-set yogurt or
   low-fat fromage frais,
   to serve

Place the redcurrants, sugar and 1 tablespoon of water in a large saucepan. Heat gently until the sugar has just dissolved and the juices have just begun to run.

Remove the saucepan from the heat and stir in the strawberries, raspberries and the Grand Marnier or Cointreau.

Line the base and sides of a 1.1 litre/2 pint pudding basin with two thirds of the bread, making sure that the slices overlap each other slightly.

Spoon the fruit with their juices into the bread-lined pudding basin, then top with the remaining bread slices.

Place a small plate on top of the pudding inside the pudding basin. Ensure the plate fits tightly, then weigh down with a clean can or some weights and chill in the refrigerator overnight.

When ready to serve, remove the weights and plate. Carefully loosen round the sides of the basin with a round-bladed knife. Invert the pudding on to a serving plate, decorate with the mint sprigs and serve with the yogurt or fromage frais.

# Caramelised Oranges
# in an Iced Bowl

**SERVES 4**

For the iced bowl:
about 36 ice cubes
fresh flowers and fruits

8 medium-sized oranges
225 g/8 oz caster sugar
4 tbsp Grand Marnier
or Cointreau

Set freezer to rapid freeze. Place a few ice cubes in the base of a 1.7 litre/3 pint freezable glass bowl. Place a 900 ml/1½ pint glass bowl on top of the ice cubes. Arrange the flower heads and fruits in between the two bowls, wedging in position with the ice cubes. Weigh down the smaller bowl with some heavy weights, then carefully pour cold water between the two bowls making sure that the flowers and the fruit are covered. Freeze for at least 6 hours or until the ice is frozen solid.

When ready to use, remove the weights and using a hot damp cloth rub the inside of the smaller bowl with the cloth until it loosens sufficiently for you to remove the bowl. Place the larger bowl in the sink or washing-up bowl, half filled with very hot water. Leave for about 30 seconds or until the ice loosens. Take care not to leave the bowl in the water for too long otherwise the ice will melt. Remove the bowl and leave in the refrigerator. Return the freezer to its normal setting.

Thinly pare the rind from two oranges and then cut into julienne strips. Using a sharp knife cut away the rind and pith from all the oranges, holding over a bowl to catch the juices. Slice the oranges, discarding any pips and reform each orange back to its original shape. Secure with cocktail sticks, then place in a bowl.

Heat 300 ml/½ pint water, orange rind and sugar together in a pan. Stir the sugar until dissolved. Bring to the boil. Boil for 15 minutes, until it is a caramel colour. Remove pan from heat. Stir in the liqueur, pour over the oranges. Allow to cool. Chill for 3 hours, turning the oranges occasionally. Spoon into the ice bowl and serve.

*Try this:* FOR STARTERS: 38   FOR MAIN MEAL: 184

# Raspberry Sorbet Crush

**SERVES 4**

225 g/8 oz raspberries,
  thawed if frozen
grated rind and juice
  of 1 lime

300 ml/½ pint orange juice
225 g/8 oz caster sugar
2 medium egg whites

Set the freezer to rapid freeze. If using fresh raspberries pick over and lightly rinse. Place the raspberries in a dish and, using a masher, mash to a chunky purée.

Place the lime rind and juice, orange juice and half the caster sugar in a large heavy-based saucepan. Heat gently, stirring frequently, until the sugar is dissolved. Bring to the boil and boil rapidly for about 5 minutes.

Remove the pan from the heat and pour carefully into a freezable container. Leave to cool, then place in the freezer and freeze for 2 hours, stirring occasionally to break up the ice crystals.

Fold the ice mixture into the raspberry purée with a metal spoon and freeze for a further 2 hours, stirring occasionally.

Whisk the egg whites until stiff. Then gradually whisk in the remaining caster sugar a tablespoon at a time until the egg white mixture is stiff and glossy.

Fold into the raspberry sorbet with a metal spoon and freeze for 1 hour. Spoon into tall glasses and serve immediately. Remember to return the freezer to its normal setting.

# Raspberry Soufflé

**SERVES 4**

| | | |
|---|---|---|
| 125 g/4 oz redcurrants | 3 medium eggs, separated | thawed if frozen |
| 50 g/2 oz caster sugar | 300 g/½ pint half-fat | To decorate: |
| 1 sachet (3 tsp) | Greek yogurt | mint sprigs |
| powdered gelatine | 450 g/1 lb raspberries, | extra fruits |

Wrap a band of double thickness greaseproof paper around four ramekin dishes, making sure that 5 cm/2 inches of the paper stays above the top of each dish. Secure the paper to the dish with an elastic band or Sellotape.

Place the redcurrants and 1 tablespoon of the sugar in a small saucepan. Cook for 5 minutes until softened. Remove from the heat, sieve and reserve.

Place 3 tablespoons of water in a small bowl and sprinkle over the gelatine. Allow to stand for 5 minutes until spongy. Place the bowl over a pan of simmering water and leave until dissolved. Remove and allow to cool.

Beat together the remaining sugar and egg yolks until pale thick and creamy, then fold in the yogurt with a metal spoon or rubber spatula until well blended.

Sieve the raspberries and fold into the yogurt mixture with the gelatine. Whisk the egg whites until stiff and fold into the yogurt mixture. Pour into the prepared dishes and chill in the refrigerator for 2 hours until firm.

Remove the paper from the dishes and spread the redcurrant purée over the top of the soufflés. Decorate with mint sprigs and extra fruits and serve.

*Try this:* FOR STARTERS: 42   FOR MAIN MEAL: 180

# Fruity Roulade

**SERVES 4**

For the sponge:
3 medium eggs
75 g/3 oz caster sugar
75 g/3 oz plain flour, sieved
1–2 tbsp caster sugar
    for sprinkling

For the filling:
125 g/4 oz Quark
125 g/4 oz half-fat
    Greek yogurt
25 g/1 oz caster sugar
1 tbsp orange
    liqueur (optional)

grated rind of 1 orange
125 g/4 oz strawberries,
    hulled and cut into quarters

To decorate:
strawberries
sifted icing sugar

Preheat the oven to 220°C/425°F/Gas Mark 7. Lightly oil and line a 33 x 23 cm/13 x 9 inch Swiss roll tin with greaseproof or baking parchment paper.

Using an electric whisk, whisk the eggs and sugar until the mixture is double in volume and leaves a trail across the top. Fold in the flour with a metal spoon or rubber spatula. Pour into the prepared tin and bake in the preheated oven for 10–12 minutes, until well risen and golden.

Place a whole sheet of greaseproof or baking parchment paper out on a flat work surface and sprinkle evenly with caster sugar.

Turn the cooked sponge out on to the paper, discard the paper, trim the sponge and roll up encasing the paper inside. Reserve until cool.

To make the filling, mix together the Quark, yogurt, caster sugar, liqueur (if using) and orange rind. Unroll the roulade and spread over the mixture. Scatter over the strawberries and roll up.

Decorate the roulade with the strawberries. Dust with the icing sugar and serve.

# Index